Women in the Modern History of Libya

Women in the Modern History of Libya features histories of Libyan women exploring the diversity of cultures, languages and memories of Libya from the age of the Empires to the present.

The chapters explore a series of institutional and private archives inside and outside Libya, illuminating historical trajectories marginalised by colonialism, nationalism and identity politics. They provide engaging and critical exploration of the archives of the Ottoman cities, of the colonial forces of Italy, Britain and the US, and of the Libyan resistance – the Mawsūʻat riwāyāt al-jihād (Oral Narratives of the Jihād) collection at the Libyan Studies Center of Tripoli – as well as of the private records in the homes of Jewish and Amazigh Libyans across the world. Developing the tools of women's and gender studies and engaging with the multiple languages of Libya, contributors raise a series of critical questions on the writing of history and on the representation of Libyan people in the past and the present.

Illuminating the sheer diversity of histories, memories and languages of Libya, *Women in the Modern History of Libya* will be of great interest to scholars of North Africa; women's and gender history; memory in history; cultural studies; and colonialism. The chapters were originally published as a special issue of the *Journal of North African Studies*.

Barbara Spadaro is Lecturer in Italian History and Culture at the University of Liverpool, UK. Her principal areas of research are the history of Italians from North Africa, colonial and postcolonial migration and transcultural memory. She has published articles and a monograph on the history of women in the Italian empire, ideas of Italian whiteness and the Jewish diaspora from Libya.

Katrina Yeaw is Assistant Professor of History at the University of Arkansas at Little Rock, USA. Her research interests include gender, race, colonialism, violence, memory, law, resistance and collaboration, and colonial and post-colonial literature.

Women in the Modern History of Libya

Exploring Transnational Trajectories

Edited by
Barbara Spadaro and Katrina Yeaw

LONDON AND NEW YORK

First published 2020
by Routledge
2 Park Square, Milton Park, Abingdon, Oxon, OX14 4RN

and by Routledge
52 Vanderbilt Avenue, New York, NY 10017

Routledge is an imprint of the Taylor & Francis Group, an informa business

© 2020 Taylor & Francis

All rights reserved. No part of this book may be reprinted or reproduced or utilised in any form or by any electronic, mechanical, or other means, now known or hereafter invented, including photocopying and recording, or in any information storage or retrieval system, without permission in writing from the publishers.

Trademark notice: Product or corporate names may be trademarks or registered trademarks, and are used only for identification and explanation without intent to infringe.

British Library Cataloguing in Publication Data
A catalogue record for this book is available from the British Library

ISBN13: 978-0-367-89424-5

Typeset in Myriad Pro
by Newgen Publishing UK

Publisher's Note
The publisher accepts responsibility for any inconsistencies that may have arisen during the conversion of this book from journal articles to book chapters, namely the inclusion of journal terminology.

Disclaimer
Every effort has been made to contact copyright holders for their permission to reprint material in this book. The publishers would be grateful to hear from any copyright holder who is not here acknowledged and will undertake to rectify any errors or omissions in future editions of this book.

Contents

Citation Information   vi
Notes on Contributors   viii

Introduction: Gender and transnational histories of Libya   1
Barbara Spadaro and Katrina Yeaw

1. Centre and periphery: variations in gendered space among Libyan Jews in the late Ottoman period   5
Rachel Simon

2. Finding women and gender in the sources: toward a historical anthropology of Ottoman Tripoli   24
Nora Lafi

3. Gender, violence and resistance under Italian rule in Cyrenaica, 1923–1934   47
Katrina Yeaw

4. Remembering the 'Italian' Jewish homes of Libya: gender and transcultural memory (1967–2013)   67
Barbara Spadaro

5. Our star: Amazigh music and the production of intimacy in 2011 Libya   90
Leila Tayeb

Index   107

Citation Information

The chapters in this book were originally published in the *Journal of North African Studies*, volume 23, issue 5 (December 2018). When citing this material, please use the original page numbering for each article, as follows:

Introduction
Gender and transnational histories of Libya
Barbara Spadaro and Katrina Yeaw
Journal of North African Studies, volume 23, issue 5 (December 2018), pp. 745–748

Chapter 1
Centre and periphery: variations in gendered space among Libyan Jews in the late Ottoman period
Rachel Simon
Journal of North African Studies, volume 23, issue 5 (December 2018), pp. 749–767

Chapter 2
Finding women and gender in the sources: toward a historical anthropology of Ottoman Tripoli
Nora Lafi
Journal of North African Studies, volume 23, issue 5 (December 2018), pp. 768–790

Chapter 3
Gender, violence and resistance under Italian rule in Cyrenaica, 1923–1934
Katrina Yeaw
Journal of North African Studies, volume 23, issue 5 (December 2018), pp. 791–810

Chapter 4
Remembering the 'Italian' Jewish homes of Libya: gender and transcultural memory (1967–2013)
Barbara Spadaro
*Journal of North African Studie*s, volume 23, issue 5 (December 2018), pp. 811–833

Chapter 5
Our star: Amazigh music and the production of intimacy in 2011 Libya
Leila Tayeb
Journal of North African Studies, volume 23, issue 5 (December 2018), pp. 834–850

For any permission-related enquiries please visit:
www.tandfonline.com/page/help/permissions

Notes on Contributors

Nora Lafi is a Postdoctoral Researcher at Leibniz-Zentrum Moderner Orient, Germany.

Rachel Simon is Head of the Middle Eastern Approvals Section at Princeton University Library, USA.

Barbara Spadaro is Lecturer in Italian History and Culture at the University of Liverpool, UK.

Leila Tayeb is Stanford H. Taylor Postdoctoral Associate in Music and Islam in the Contemporary World in the Department of Music at Cornell University, USA.

Katrina Yeaw is Assistant Professor of History at the University of Arkansas at Little Rock, USA.

INTRODUCTION

Gender and transnational histories of Libya

Barbara Spadaro and Katrina Yeaw

This series of articles focuses on Libya to investigate how individual and collective identities are imagined, experienced, and narrated in a mobile and interconnected world. Drawing from original and unexplored sources in seven different languages, our case studies illuminate subjects and circuits long neglected from historiography, and yet crucial for the understanding of the transnational and transcultural memory of Libya. Our critical engagement with ways in which histories of Libya have been materialised, colonised, regimented and forgotten reflects a wider shift across the academic discipline of History.

Historians who works on the entangled social and cultural histories of the Middle East, North Africa and the Mediterranean are living 'an important historiographical moment, in which the major categories, historical narratives, and key assumption within the field are undergoing radical changes' (Bashkin 2014, 577). This new scholarly wave, as identified by Bashkin, has three main features: it is transnational, as it explores and draws comparisons between networks and languages across transregional areas; 'it is interdisciplinary, in its attempt to incorporate the insights of sociologists, anthropologists and literary scholars. Finally, it is postcolonial, in its critiques to national elites, national narratives, and nationalist histories' (Bashkin 2014, 577).

Stretching from the late Ottoman period to the present, our case studies highlight subjects and sites of the transnational, diasporic and multilingual history of Libya. Our perspective engages with the power dynamics that casted early historical narratives and that keep shaping ideas of history and belonging. Our investigation begins with the mid-nineteenth century, exploring the moment of the geopolitical construction of Libya via imperial and Eurocentric categories that have been translated, and contested by scholars and historical subjects over time. It then moves on to the colonial period, which witnessed the shattering of existing forms of subjectivity and the construction of new understandings of gender under Italian rule. Finally, it addresses the postcolonial era and takes up recent developments in Libya since the upheaval of the 2010 uprising from North Africa.

While addressing a relatively long historical period, our case studies all tackle the mobility of people, objects, languages and representations across the Mediterranean and the Atlantic, exploring how individual and collective identities are constructed across cultures, and mediated over time. Each article focuses on a specific microcosm of these dynamics: the chronicles of Ottoman cities, the scattered groups of *mujahidin* resistance, the houses of Jewish families 'repatriated' to the colonial metropole of Rome. These sites are spaces in which the relational construction of gendered and racialized identities occurs via multiple acts of transmission over time. Our contributions tease out the power dynamics of memory examining a diverse range of materials, from archival records to contemporary mnemonic practices. The articles consider the mediation and circulation of Oral History collections, family albums, and contemporary music. Featuring the movements of visual, written and aural narratives in a variety of languages, this collection aims to highlight the multiple circuits of cultural mobility in which memory and history of Libya travel.

Libya remains one of the least understood and theorised regions in the Middle Eastern and North Africa, and to date no publications on women and gender have targeted the region. A remarkable exception is Rachel Simon's pioneer scholarship on the history of Jewish Women in Libya (Simon 1992). Rachel Simon has joined us for the seminar *Gendering the History of Libya: Transnational and Feminist Approaches* convened by Barbara Spadaro and Elisabetta Bini at the 2014 Berkshire Conference of Women Historians in Toronto, and her work is featured in this collection.[1] Beyond filling a gap in historical research by digging out histories of women (and men!) who lived, travelled and carry memories of Libya, our aim has been to raise awareness of conversations on the reading and writing of History that are happening across multiple academic fields. To put it in the words of our discussant, Julia Clancy-Smith, this is an important task 'not only for the many histories of Libya but also for those of North Africa, the Middle East, and Europe and for the study of women, gender, and empire globally and comparatively' (Clancy-Smith 2015).

This collection takes further the transnational and cultural approaches to the study of History that we authors share as a new generation of scholars of North African, European and North American backgrounds. Our work builds on pioneering scholarship on transnational and diasporic histories (Pergher 2007; Stein 2008; Baldinetti 2010; Proglio 2016). As early career scholars wrestling with the resistance of epistemological frameworks and of linguistic and disciplinary boundaries, we have been changing trajectories and experimenting research strategies, questioning our practice of historians.

Our early research questions about subjects marginalised by mainstream narratives of Italian, Libyan, Arab, Amazigh, Muslim, Jewish, French belonging have been driven by Gender and Postcolonial Studies and Transnational History. Feminist intersectional methodology has inspired our multidimensional reading of identities, whether centred on religious, gendered, ethnic or national processes of identifications. Memory Studies have enriched our questions on the uses and practices of History in this age of accelerated, digitalised and travelling memories (Erll 2011). Literary scholars have raised our awareness of power and translation with their invite to 'knowing the world through languages' (Pratt 2003). In the long process of editing and publishing this series of articles, the exhibitions curated by Najlaa El-Ageli as Noon Arts Project (https://www.noonartsprojects.com/) have been showing the potential of Arts and curatorial practices to propel research questions on transcultural memory and history. As new avenues for research on the media of history of Libya are opening, the scholarship in this collection enter multiple territories and languages connecting past, present, and futures.

Note

1. Three of the articles in this collection were first presented at the seminar *Gendering the History of Libya: Transnational and Feminist Approaches* convened by Barbara Spadaro and Elisabetta Bini at the 2014 Berkshire Conference of Women Historians in Toronto, Canada. The editors wish to acknowledge the participation to the discussion in Toronto of fellow panelists whose work is not featured in this publication: Elisabetta Bini, Jennifer Illuzzi, Tommaso Palmieri. Thanks to Amy Kallander for chairing the panel, and to Julia Clancy-Smith for her generous engagement as discussant.

Disclosure statement

No potential conflict of interest was reported by the authors.

References

Baldinetti, Anna. 2010. *The Origins of the Libyan Nation. Colonial Legacy, Exile and the Emergency of a New Nation-State*. London: Routledge.
Bashkin, Orit. 2014. "The Middle Eastern Shift and Provincializing Zionism." *International Journal of Middle East Studies* 46 (3): 577–580. doi:10.1017/S0020743814000609.
Clancy-Smith, Julia. 2015. "Review Essay: Gendering the History of Libya: Transnational and Feminist Approaches." *Journal of Middle East Women's Studies* 11 (1): 98–103.
Erll, Astrid. 2011. "Travelling Memory." *Parallax* 17 (4): 4–18. doi:10.1080/13534645.2011.605570.
Pergher, Roberta. 2007. "A Tale of Two Borders: Settlement and National Transformation in Libya and South Tyrol Under Fascism." PhD diss., University of Michigan.

Pratt, Mary Louise. 2003. "Building a New Public Idea About Language." *Profession* 2003 (1): 110–119. doi:10.1632/074069503X85472.
Proglio, Gabriele. 2016. *Libia 1911-1912: Immaginari Coloniali e Italianità. Quaderni Di Storia*. Firenze: Le Monnier.
Simon, Rachel. 1992. *Change Within Tradition among Jewish Women in Libya*. Seattle: University of Washington Press.
Stein, Sarah Abrevaya. 2008. *Plumes: Ostrich Feathers, Jews, and a Lost World of Global Commerce*. New Haven: Yale University Press.

Centre and periphery: variations in gendered space among Libyan Jews in the late Ottoman period

Rachel Simon

ABSTRACT
To what an extent did 'women space' among Libyan Jews refer only to the home and a secluded female environment? Were there any inter-gender contacts except for those among close family relatives? This article examines gendered space among Libyan Jews in the late Ottoman period (mid-nineteenth to early twentieth centuries) in the urban coastal centres and the rural hinterland. It shows that the answers to these questions varied depending on locale, socioeconomic status, foreign influence, cultural development, and the passage of time. The available data indicates that the further one was from the geographical and political 'centre' and the lower one's socioeconomic status, the wider the space each gender held, the more flexible and blurred its boundaries, and the greater the possibilities for inter-gender contacts. The study also explores the elasticity of gendered space and how various groups viewed it, as well as its economic, social and communal rationale, based on indigenous and foreign sources. While the sources, which were mostly composed by men, focus on Jews, it is highly likely that the situation among the Muslim majority and in the region in general was similar.

To what an extent did 'women space' among Libyan Jews refer only to the home and a secluded female environment? Were there any inter-gender contacts except for those among close family relatives? This article examines gendered space among Libyan Jews in the late Ottoman period (mid-nineteenth to early twentieth centuries) in the urban coastal centres and the rural hinterland. It shows that the answers to these questions varied depending on locale, socioeconomic status, foreign influence, cultural development, and the passage of time. The available data indicates that the further one was from the geographical and political 'centre' and the lower one's socioeconomic status, the wider the space each gender held, the more flexible and blurred its boundaries, and the greater the possibilities for inter-gender contacts. The study also explores the elasticity of gendered space and how various groups viewed it, as well as its economic, social and communal rationale, based on indigenous and foreign sources. While the sources, which were mostly composed by men, focus on Jews, it is highly likely that the situation among the Muslim majority and in the region in general was similar.

Body bounds

One manifestation of inter-gender relations is the attitude towards the body. This is reflected in the way people dress, how they deal with intimate apparel, and how the body and its functions are treated. Various customs and regulations were set to ensure women's chastity and segregation, yet social, economic, and cultural pressures could at times bring about some easing of these rules.

When women[1] ventured outside the home, they had to cover themselves with a sheet so that no part of the body, except for one eye, could be easily discerned, especially by strange men. This practice was explained as a means to prevent lasciviousness (*zimah*) (Hacohen 1978, 47).[2] Jewish women used their clothing to distinguish themselves from the general population in several ways. They used to wear, for example, a cap embroidered with silver threads and silk diadems on their forehead, which totally concealed their hair. In addition, they wore wide sleeves made of silk, and covered their chest and neck with a vest made of silver bars in the form of buds and flowers. Over the vest women wore a long silk coat (*kaftan*) embroidered with silver threads, covering the neck, chest and arms, and a red silk or woollen sheet wrapped around their body (Hacohen 1978, 47–48). As a result, women's faces were hardly seen and the shapes of their bodies were hidden. On various occasions, they wore special garments. Thus, on *Yom Kippur*, the Jewish Day of Atonement, they covered themselves with a white sheet and the girls wore elegant attire (Hacohen 1978, 192).

Until the early eighteenth century women in Libya did not wear pantalets, because it would have been considered shameful, and they covered their thighs with a sheet. The notable Shelomoh Khalfon was the first to break this habit when in 1732 he gave his daughter Aziza a pair of pantalets as part of her dowry. Gradually, this fashion spread although pantalets remained a garment of the private domain, and women took special precautions when they laundered them (Hacohen 1978, 48, 291). By the beginning of the twentieth century, it became more customary for women to wear pantalets, their shirt sleeves had narrowed, and they replaced caps with scarves to cover their hair. Many men, women and children started wearing bootlegs, something that was unheard of before (Hacohen 1978, 48). As a result, the public, including non-related men, could see the women's faces as well as make up the shape of their bodies. Socioeconomic conventions further eased these dress codes in the rural society, where women had to perform several physical tasks outside the home. In other words, outside the cities, women's clothing was better suited to work requirements than to constraints of modesty: they had to have their arms free, be able to move easily, and have nothing block their sight (Simon 1992, 29–33).

Until the end of the nineteenth century urban women took special care in drying their laundered intimate apparel: they did not dry their pantalets in the sun for everyone to see, but only behind closed doors. This, however, changed over time, and in the twentieth century women started to dry them in the open, spread in the sun (Hacohen 1978, 48). Thus, not only could men have an idea how women's bodies looked like, but they could also get a glimpse of women's apparel, which suggesting intimate contact was unheard of in previous times.

Bathing was usually done in private and mostly for ritual purity purposes rather than for hygienic concerns. According to Jewish law, women are considered impure during menstruation or after giving birth, and they can purify themselves only by immersing themselves in a *mikveh* (ritual bath), which is a required institution in a Jewish community, because only following the ritual purification does Jewish law allow a couple to resume sexual relations. Furthermore, Jewish law requires women to wait seven 'clean' days following menstruation. The regulations were even more strict following giving birth: it was customary in Libya that women wait forty days following the birth of a boy and eighty days following the birth of a girl, before they could purify themselves, namely, a woman was considered twice as impure following the birth of a girl as after giving birth to a boy. Thus, according to the customs prevailing in Libya, every month, during a period of about ten to fourteen days, the husband was forbidden to touch his wife or have any physical contact with her, even by throwing objects to her. In some Libyan villages the husband would not even step on a mat that his menstruating wife had stepped on, nor did he even look at her or talk with her except for the most essential matters, and then only in short and quick manner. In the early twentieth century, some urban women became less strict regarding purification regulations, and while they still went to the *mikveh*, they did so immediately after the bleeding stopped without waiting the customary number of clean days (Hacohen 1978, 252, 272, 285, 300, 304, 317, 320, 329).

Women usually went to the *mikveh* in the evening. They used public spring or rainwater *mikvehs*, and some wealthy Jews had a private *mikveh* at home. In 1913 several public *mikvehs* had heated water (Hacohen 1978, 252, 272). In some small places, the *mikvehs* were in poor shape, such as that in the village Disir in Jebel Nefusa region in Central Tripolitania, which had turbid and stinking water during the summer (Hacohen 1978, 297). Some small communities did not even have a *mikveh* at all: this, for example, was the case in Zanzur, and as a result women had to immerse themselves in the sea (Hacohen 1978, 319). This, obviously, raises the issue of privacy and modesty, as well as the extent to which the male-dominant community leadership was actually trying to ease the purification process for the women.

In addition to a purification following menstruation and childbirth, women went to the *mikveh* on other occasions. For example, many people – both men (with separate hours for each gender) and women – went to the *mikveh* to purify themselves prior to the Three Festivals of Pilgrimage (Passover, Pentecost and Tabernacles), as well as on the eves of *Yamim nora'im* (High Holidays) (Hacohen 1978, 252). Moreover, going to the *mikveh* was not only for washing and purification purposes: a bride would go to the *mikveh* on the eve of her wedding, and female relatives of the bridegroom accompanied her and furtively check if she had any bodily blemishes (Hacohen 1978, 275; there is no mention of a similar inspection of bridegrooms).

Jewish women in Libya had special regulations regarding washing and wearing clean clothing following the *shiv'ah* (seven prescribed days of mourning for a close relative) and the Ninth of Av Fast (commemorating the destruction of the Second Temple of Jerusalem). Following the *shiv'ah*, women wore clothing cleaned in water but without the use of natron (a substance which they usually used for laundry) (Hacohen 1978, 207). When the mourning period was over, women customarily washed in warm water, because it was difficult to comb their hair after washing it in cold water. Consequently, when the last day of mourning fell on the Sabbath, the Jewish day of rest, women extended it for a day, so that they would be able to heat water (considered 'work' on the Sabbath) and wash their hair. It was even forbidden to wash in water which was kept warm from Friday (Hacohen 1978, 219–220; Hacohen regarded this custom of extending the mourning period as stupid).

Sanitary provisions were rare in most Libyan homes until the twentieth century. Thus, for example, for the lack of latrines, people in Jebel Nefusa, used to relieve themselves in the early hours of the day in the field in special empty places, and then clean themselves with stones (Hacohen 1978, 291). No mention is made as to whether there were designated areas for men and women. Towards the end of the Ottoman period, with the greater attention of the state to public health and municipal improvements, the authorities created for themselves and for the inhabitants of Tripoli special restrooms, with ditches from which the waste rolled out to an external large pit (Hacohen 1978, 291). In Mislata, meanwhile, every house had a cavern serving as a toilet, because they did not relieve themselves in the fields as was done in Yefren and Gharian (Hacohen 1978, 321).

Women's work

In principle, women's work was confined to the home. Yet the definition of 'home' and 'home related work' had different meanings in urban and rural settings, with a broader definition for the latter. Certain tasks were traditionally considered 'women's work': grinding flour, baking, laundry, cooking, spinning wool, making sheets and carpets, drawing water and chopping wood (Hacohen 1978, 308–309). In addition, some occupations were restricted to women because they dealt with the female body. Economic necessity, however, required women at times to work outside their homes for tasks not related to their family. But even in both latter categories, it was preferred that women work in an all-female environment, although this was not always possible.

Preparing food for the family and guests was a female task, and women were often praised for their industrious and fast work (Hacohen 1978, 194, 290). A subsidiary of this task was grinding flour. Women using hand mills usually ground flour at home, in private, at dawn, often accompanying their grinding with special songs. In the early twentieth century, some places had camel-driven mills operated by Muslim men, but many women continued to grind their daily supply at home (Hacohen 1978, 308). It is possible that it was hard to break with tradition, or, by going to the camel-driven mills, women might have to interact with men who were not kin. Going to the camel-driven mill also required some sort of payment, whereas grinding at home was 'free', namely, it required 'only' women's time and labour.

In the Jewish month of Nissan women had to comply with the particular Passover regulations, which forbid any leavened goods. Since this festival commences in the middle of Nissan, women ground a two-week supply of flour at the beginning of the month for the days prior to Passover. They then had to properly clean the mills, following which they prepared special flour for Passover, which extends for seven days (Hacohen 1978, 302). In Mislata, however, grinding flour for Passover was done only in the camel-driven mills, while during the rest of the year it was done both there and at home (Hacohen 1978, 322).

Food was always prepared ahead of time for the Sabbath, but keeping it warm and in good shape was difficult at times. Rabbis used to complain that when women saw that the dish that had been kept warm from Friday became cold they brought it to be re-warmed at an oven operated by gentiles (Hacohen 1978, 213). Thus, although the women themselves did not work on the Sabbath, they made others work for them, and came in contact with gentile, unrelated men.

Laundry was also one of the women's tasks. In Jebel Nefusa they did their laundry infrequently: every three months or in preparation for the holidays (Hacohen 1978, 292).

In the rural areas, it was much more common than in town for women to work outside the house. The distance from the house varied and at times their work required that they not only could, but often should have worked even at a great distance from home. Most of the women's daily work, though, was in the garden next to their house, while their children played around them.

There they did some agricultural work, including plowing and harvesting, beating olive trees in order to get the olives off the trees and make olive oil, and raising chicken for eggs (Hacohen 1978, 309).

Women were also involved in agricultural surplus trade, which could bring them in contact with non-kin men. In 1886, the scholar and merchant Mordecai Hacohen started to buy chicken eggs from a Jewish woman in Jebel Yefren, whose husband was often absent on business for long periods of time, like many Jewish peddlers in the region. She started this business because she barely had enough to feed her children, but did not receive any charity from the community, as communal-sponsored charity was not customary in that region. Hacohen offered to pay her twice the price of eggs, and while this enabled her to make some money, he could still sell the eggs for a profit in Tripoli (Hacohen 1978, 288). This example suggests that rural women had no difficulty coming into contact with non-kin men. It is also known that Jewish peddlers had direct contact not only with Jewish women but with Muslim women as well (Hacohen 1978, 286; Simon 1993, 294–296). The transaction between Hacohen and the Jebel Yefren woman also shows that business dealings could be in both directions, namely, that local inhabitants sold produce to peddlers and bought merchandise from them. And indeed, there were Jewish rural women who were involved in trade (e.g. in Mislata). Hacohen points out that business dealings between rural women and peddlers did on occasion lead some women to licentiousness (Hacohen 1978, 322). It is not stated whether the women of Mislata traded at home or took their produce to the local market place or even further to neighbouring villages. Nor is it clear whether Hacohen's remark concerning the morality of the local female traders represents an urban point of view or if it was common local view. One should remember that in this region many men were often away peddling for a long period of time – at times even returning home only twice a year for the High Holidays and Passover. Since numerous men were away on business for lengthy periods of time, this might have had implications on family life, and might have aroused suspicions regarding the morality of the women left behind without male guardianship, except for that of the older male members of the extended family.

Some tasks required rural women to go considerably beyond the boundaries their homes; these included regular tasks, like the drawing of water and chopping wood as well as the sporadic hewing of natron, which could be rather dangerous. Drawing water was usually done daily and within the village boundaries or in close proximity. In Jebel Nefusa the village had three wells, two of which belonged to the Berbers and one, called Baisi, belonged to the Jews. Young women used to go in the evening with a jug on their shoulder to draw all their family's water needs for a day. The wells were not deep, and in dry years, when the springs were poor, and especially during the summer, the women had to stay from daybreak till night to draw water in an orderly fashion and fill their jugs (Hacohen 1978, 306). On the night preceding Passover they went to draw all their needs for the whole holiday week (Hacohen 1978, 303). It seems that not all villages had special wells for Jews, as was the case in Khoms, where all the population used one ancient well, called al-Hasi (Hacohen 1978, 323). This meant that Jewish and Muslim women would gather at the well, and as is evident from other sources, this female gathering attracted men to the area. Thus, since due to work and life style requirements the well was a legitimate public space outside the home to frequent, it was also acceptable that men be around.

Some places used only rainwater for their daily needs and each house had to dig a cistern to gather water (e.g. in Mislata) (Hacohen 1978, 321). In Tripoli, too, they used rainwater or bought water brought on camels from wells outside the city. In 1882 the Ottoman governor Ahmet Rasim Paşa built a steam pump to draw water in Bu Meliana and transport it in pipes to al-Khandak in Tripoli, where people could get it for free. Additional pools were set up later, as was done in 1907 when a pool was built beside the town walls adjacent to the Jewish neighbourhood (Hacohen 1978, 169). No specific mention is made, though, of who participated in the transaction of water in Tripoli. It is most likely that the water carried on camels' backs was brought by Muslim men. Furthermore, since most urban men worked outside the home, it is likely that women, who stayed at home, were the ones who bought the water from the Muslim water carriers, just as some women bought merchandise from male peddlers (Hacohen 1978, 275). On the other hand, in town it was the men who usually did the household shopping in the market place, so it is likely that they also brought the water from the newly established pools. Thus, an occupation that in the rural areas was an exclusive female task might have become confined to men in town yet might also have resulted in contact between urban women at home with men who were not their kin.

Drawing water was conducted in specific places, often close to the village, where men and women used to gather. Chopping wood, however, required rural women to wander outside the village on various directions, usually on a weekly basis. In Jebel Nefusa groups of women left early each Friday morning, scattered barefoot on thorny ground far into the woods. Sometimes they had to walk for two hours in order to chop enough wood for all their baking and cooking needs for a week. At noon they returned home, each balancing a bundle of timber weighing some 50 kg on her head. In the rural context no one would have associated this task with impropriety, since there it was considered as an important task that women are required to perform. It was, however, viewed quite differently in the urban community, where women were not in charge of supplying timber for cooking and heating. The *dayanim* (judges in the Jewish court of law) in Tripoli issued a ruling against this practice, threatening the women with excommunication, in order to stop them from venturing into the woods and the fields unaccompanied and unsupervised by men. The women, however, ignored this ruling, because had they followed it and stopped ensuring the regular supply of timber, they would have been regarded by rural men and women alike as lazy, and they could not stand the shame associated with this. The women further claimed that the ruling was unjust, since previous rabbis had not prohibited the custom (Hacohen 1978, 309). Most likely, rural men – those who remained in the village and were not away peddling – were not ready to perform a task which was considered a woman's task, nor were they interested in walking out with them in order to supervise them. Thus, while one group viewed an activity as a required one, another regarded it as forbidden.

Another task, which was more sporadic, required women to wander outside the village and was connected to laundry. Instead of soap they often used for laundry a substance made of natron, which the women themselves had to fetch. Hewing natron required rural women to leave their homes unattended by men. This could even endanger their life, as was the case in Jebel Nefusa where they used to hew it from a special cave, which the mountain collapsed upon in 1889 when the women got out of it, leaving some of them injured and one dead (Hacohen 1978, 292, 308).

Services aimed at women were apparently performed only by women. Consequently, although there were male physicians in Libya, it was customary that women treated women. Midwifery was confined to women, who learned it from each other and did not possess any formal diploma until the Italian period (Hacohen 1978, 46). Cosmeticians, too, especially those beautifying brides, were women, and this occupation was usually in Jewish hands (Simon 1992, 92). Thus, women's space was maintained as regards services pertaining to the body.

In the urban sector, poverty required women, usually the young and the unmarried, to seek paid work outside their home. At first this did not alter the range of occupations carried out by women. Most poor women were maids who performed regular housework tasks in the homes of wealthier families: they either returned home in the evening or lived with their employers (Simon 1992, 95–97). Although the Jewish community preferred that Jewish maids work in Jewish homes and in female environment, this was not always possible. Still, it seems that employers felt obligated to protect these maids. Thus, for example, in 1876, when Ottoman naval cadets insulted a Jewish maid in the service of the US consul in Tripoli while she worked in his orchard, he rushed to her protection, in what evolved into a diplomatic incident (Hacohen 1978, 157). In the late nineteenth century, many Jewish maidens worked in the ostrich-feather industry, usually in an all-female environment (Simon 1992, 98–99). Women who became teachers at the same time taught mainly toddlers and girls (the latter in segregated schools

– though there were also some men who taught girls) (Simon 1992, 102–104). Thus, most wage-earning women worked in an all-female environment, the main exception being hospital nurses (but this took place only under Italian and British rule) Among the indigenous population, Muslim women for a long time did not work as nurses (Simon 1992, 101–102).

Inter-gender contacts

Inter-gender relations differed among kin and non-kin: women were not supposed to be in contact with non-related men and when they had to, they were supposed to cover their faces. But even within the family there was at times some separation. Thus, meals were usually taken separately by men and women, with the men eating first (Simon 1992, 24–25). In the rural area (e.g. Jebel Nefusa) people ate two meals a day, in the morning and at night. All men ate together and when they finished the women ate in private what was left in the pot: it was regarded as shameful and disgraceful for women to eat with men (Hacohen 1978, 289). In Tripoli, too, this was usually the custom, even in the 1940s (Simon 1992, 25). On certain occasions they changed their habits. Thus, in the early twentieth century, the rich in Tripoli, many of whom were influenced by European social practices, had their Sabbath breakfast at midday with men and women eating together at the table (Hacohen 1978, 190).

Since the work of rural women required them to perform certain tasks outside their home, they had several occasions to meet men who were not members of their close family. The most prominent inter-gender rural meeting place was at the well, which witnessed daily gatherings of the village community as well as strangers. It is likely that since the population of the village was often of an extended family, mixed gender meeting in this setting was not frowned upon. Moreover, since the well was a central place and people gathered there regularly and in the open, everyone could see and hear what everyone else was doing, and there was no fear of improper behaviour. The occasions on which young women went to draw water, and at times had to stay there for a lengthy period of time, were known and became an opportunity for men to observe them. And indeed, it was not unusual for men to choose a woman by the well and then have their families arrange the marriage (Hacohen 1978, 305).

The fact that rural women did not hesitate to interact with non-related men in public places is further demonstrated in the following event. Once, as the Tripolitan scholar-merchant Mordecai Hacohen was in Jebel Nefusa, he met a Jewish woman who was drawing water from the well. He asked her to give him some water to drink, and at first she yelled at him, retreated, and refused to respond. It later turned out that her behaviour resulted from the fact that she thought he was in mourning, and it was customary in that region not to talk with mourners. Once she realised who he was, she apologised, was ready to talk with him and gave him water, despite the fact that they were not related (Hacohen 1978, 310).

Funerals and mourning events served as public occasions during which men and women would mix. The rabbis tried to put some constraints on these meetings, or at least have only close female relatives be present. The rabbis also debated where the women should stand (whether in front or behind the coffin), and tried to limit women visiting and comforting other women in mourning (Hacohen 1978, 218–219). When the mourners took the coffin out of the deceased's house, women holding sticks encircled it and beat it loudly. One woman would be wailing and her friends followed suit, wearing kerchiefs over their uncombed heads, beating their breasts, scratching their flesh until it bled, dancing and forming groups to express their great sorrow, although this was contrary to religious practice. The female relatives of the dead would come together, each two hugging, their heads on their friend's shoulder, yelling loudly, mentioning the dead person's qualities. For example, if the deceased was learned, they would say: 'Oh, the Torah reader, ai-ai-ai-ai-ai', or 'Beloved by the people, ai-ai-ai-ai-ai'. When Italy occupied Libya, the government banned some of these practices, though in the urban centres women's wailing was permitted, but only in the cemetery (Hacohen 1978, 244, 309–310). There women would weep and prostrate themselves on the graves of their relatives. Sometimes the kerchief with which they used to cover their heads would fall, and due to their great grief, they did not notice that they were unkempt (Hacohen 1978, 246).

While there were more ceremonies commemorating deceased men than honouring deceased women, some practices were performed for both genders. They used to pray *Shaharit, Minhah* and *'Arvit* (the three daily prayers in the morning, afternoon and evening) at the house of the deceased – be it a man or a woman – during the whole week of mourning, including Monday and Thursday, the days on which the Torah is read. In addition, a rabbi gave there a sermon each evening between the afternoon and evening prayers (Hacohen 1978, 219). Then, for a year, they would pray *'Arvit* on every Sabbath's eve and at the end of the Sabbath at the home of the deceased, but by the early twentieth century this custom was somewhat neglected (Hacohen 1978, 204).

Several holiday celebrations brought women to the public sphere. One such occasion in Tripoli was the Purim festival (which takes place on the Jewish month of Adar) during which women celebrated in public. On 13 of that month boys went out with their male teacher, and each boy brought with him a figurine with a head, hands and legs made of olive tree roots, referred to as Haman (the villain of the Purim story). They tossed all these figurines in a bonfire and each mother contributed a bundle of timber in honour of her son. Many women, children and the boys' teacher surrounded the fire, singing mockingly in disgrace of Haman as flames licked the figurines. Soon after, they checked if all the figurines had burned, and broke what was left into pieces to ensure that now everything would completely burn (Hacohen 1978, 302). On another occasion, on Yom Kippur, all women covered themselves with a white sheet and accompanied with elegantly dresses girls played and sang in front of the mixed crowd by the synagogue (Hacohen 1978, 192).

Women also used to encourage communal heroes. Until the late nineteenth century it was customary for the group of Tripolitan Jewish volunteer strongmen (*biryonim*), the unofficial protectors of the community against attacks by Muslims, to conduct weekly competitive wrestling games on the Sabbath on the city wall adjacent to the Jewish quarter, with a large crowd, of men, women and children, watching the contest between two groups of the strongmen (Hacohen 1978, 119). No mention was made of separating the crowd by gender. During the 1940s, following the organisation of a Jewish defense group in Tripoli, Jewish women incited Jewish men to fight and attack rioting Arabs and at times their shouts caused the rioters to flee from the Jewish neighbourhoods (Simon 2001, 123). This behaviour was not unusual among women in Libya: in 1856 the daughter of the Berber rebel chief Ghoma encouraged the insurgent Berber men during their rebellion against the Ottomans in Tripolitania (Hacohen 1978, 144) and another Berber woman died doing another Berber rebellion against the Ottomans in 1901 (Hacohen 1978, 174).

While women were not part of the communal leadership, at least two eighteenth century women were involved in politics, even outside the Jewish community. Esther Arbib ('Queen Esther', died 1800), the wife of a communal leader, had strong contacts with the harem of the paşa of Tripoli Ali Qaramanli and eventually with the paşa himself, over whom she had great influence. She was 'considered the head of the Jewish nation, as all favours or petitions granted to the Jews by the Bashaw are only obtained from the sovereign through her influence'. She and her daughter Mezeltobe, conspired to secure the succession of Ali's youngest son, Yusuf, instead of his two elder brothers, whom they detested (Tully 1957, 180, 268, 362–363; Simon 1992, 200–201).

Courting and marital life

Arranged marriages were the norm in Libya where the families of the couple were usually the ones to decide on the match, yet the young had some say in the matter. In the rural areas it was relatively easy for young men and women to meet. Most of the village population belonged to the same extended family, and thus they could meet in family gatherings, especially during holidays and special occasions. In addition, the well served as a neutral meeting point (Hacohen 1978, 305), especially as men knew that young women went there to draw water at predetermined times and in the summer occasionally had to stay there for a lengthy period of time. Thus, the youth had occasions to meet and voice their marriage preferences, but marriage arrangements themselves were the responsibility of the families of the couple. When a young Jewish man in the countryside felt things were not going his way, he would at times ask the Muslim protector of the village Jews to help him get the maiden against her father's wish, and he usually succeeded in his endeavour (Hacohen 1978, 314). Thus, not only were the young at times able to impose their marriage preferences upon their parents, but the non-Jewish leadership might also be involved in the process, as shown by the above example.

In rural areas like Jebel Nefusa it was customary that once a girl was asked in marriage, the betrothed couple would not meet face to face until the wedding. Thus, when the woman heard her bridegroom coming, she would cover her face with the 'Veil of shame' (Hacohen 1978, 306). The separation went even further once the wedding festivities had started. By then, custom required that the girl feel a sense of shame even before her parents and would escape to find shelter with one of her female relatives. She covered herself with the 'Veil of shame', which was hiding her face, and she would not meet anyone until the wedding (Hacohen 1978, 306). The bridegroom, too, had to leave his father's house, accompanied by one of his male friends, referred to as *shushbin*, who would watch over him during the entire wedding festivities (Hacohen 1978, 306). Some rural men, who were influenced by urban practices, gradually brought about changes in this custom. For example, a rural man from Yefren who was raised in Tripoli by Mordecai Hacohen, returned home to get married. He did not run away from his parents' house prior to the wedding festivities and the local people were gossiping about this, how he was not ashamed not to flee from his parents' house. The bridegroom, however, did not pay attention to the crowd, and remarked: 'why should I flee, am I a thief?' (Hacohen 1978, 306).

On the day following the wedding, the bridegroom in Jebel Nefusa was forbidden to leave his home because on this day he was required to remain with his wife and make her happy. It was customary that for one month following the wedding the bridegroom would not enter a room in which both his wife and his parents were present (Hacohen 1978, 307). It is possible that this separation of the newly wed couple from the husband's parents (in whose house they lived) reflected some embarrassment regarding their sexual union.

Inter-gender encounters were more difficult in the urban setting than in the village. In Tripoli Jewish maidens would not meet any non-kin young men face to face, and they used to cover their face with the 'Veil of shame' when meeting non-kin men. The women would say only the most necessary to the men and speak softly. This was especially so for betrothed women: when they heard the footsteps of the bridegroom, they would run away as from a snake. The couple would meet face to face only during the 'Seven Blessings' at the wedding ceremony. By the early twentieth century, however, it did happen that women took off the 'Veil of shame' and the betrothed couple would meet and talk face to face. The more traditional in the community frowned upon this, saying that even if no sin was committed, sinful thoughts might have passed (Hacohen 1978, 274–275).

Some men were worried that they would not like the prospective bride and made arrangements to see her before becoming engaged during an event known as a '*tagliya*', or revelation, when the woman 'revealed' herself. The man would send to the bride's father's house meat and all that was needed for a festive meal, which was attended by the bridegroom's relatives. The bride's parents would ensure that their daughter dress well and appear at her best before the bridegroom on this occasion during which he could see her face. If he liked her, the betrothal (*shidukhin*) would take place. This practice, though, was despicable, because had he not approved, she was left to feel great shame (Hacohen 1978, 275). It is not mentioned, and seems unlikely, that a woman had a similar prerogative to reject a man chosen by her parents on the same grounds. Some men were quite ingenious in their attempts to see their prospective bride. For example, one man had contrived to see the girl by dressing like a gardener, carrying a bundle of turnips as if for sale, and strolling in front of her house. She came out dressed in her dowdy house clothes and bought the turnips from him, upon which he said that although she was wearing rags, he could see how beautiful she was. The embarrassed girl ran away, but on the same night he asked to marry her (Hacohen 1978, 275).

The Jews of Tripoli came up with an annual event which enabled men to observe marriageable young women in public. This occasion took place on the afternoon of the last day of Passover, when young women, with their faces exposed, beautified themselves, put on their prettiest garments and jewellery and stood at the window, on the balcony or even outside the gate of their homes, while young men sauntered to watch the maidens. If a man saw a woman he liked, all the other men and women threw flowers in front of the couple. Consequently, this day was referred to as the Festival of the Roses (*Hag ha-shoshanim*). Then, on the same evening, the young man would communicate his intentions to the girl's parents by bringing them a basket full of lettuce and flowers: the acceptance of the present meant the consent of the parents to the marriage proposal. This event was called Lettuce and Flowers (*khass wa-nuwwar*) (Simon 1992, 48). Due to the restrictions on inter-gender interactions and the fact that marriages were usually arranged by the parents, it is likely that this event was meant to enable urban young men to observe their future brides at a public setting after marriage had already been discussed by the families but before any formal agreement has been reached.

There were several all-female pre-wedding celebrations, such as the Sabbath of the Girls (*Sabbat al-banat*) when the bride met her girlfriends (Hacohen 1978, 275). This was followed by the *hena* ceremony, when women beautified the bride by painting her face, hands and feet with the earthy red dye *hena* (Hacohen 1978, 53, 306). The wedding ceremony was usually conducted at the bridegroom's parents' house (Hacohen 1978, 220) where the young couple later lived. Since in Libya, as in other Muslim countries, it was allowed for Jewish men to marry a second wife, some Jewish men from Europe, whose wives remained childless, came to Libya to marry a second wife (Hacohen 1978, 117, 231).

Divorce is permitted by Jewish law, but the *dayanim* in Libya used to be slow in processing it, hoping for reconciliation. If, however, there was any suggestion of adultery on the woman's part, the Jewish court of law would make a concerted effort to speed up divorce. When a man divorced his wife against her will, he had to add a sixth to the sum which had been agreed upon in their marriage contact (*ketubah*). In addition, he could not marry another wife without the first wife's agreement. If, however, they were married for ten years and she had borne no children, he could divorce her without adding a sixth to the sum agreed upon in the *ketubah* or marry another woman but with the first wife's consent (Hacohen 1978, 202–203, 207–209).

While the Jewish community made great efforts at maintaining gender separation among non-related men and women, extra-marital sex did occur, and it was usually the woman who was punished. When the community caught a Jewish prostitute or an adulteress, she was beaten with a stick, her hair was shaved and was tied to a long pole which was carried with great fanfare through the streets of the Jewish neighbourhoods by the Talmud Torah students to publicise her disgraceful doings (Hacohen 1978, 255).[3]

In Ottoman Tripoli, as elsewhere, political power could have an impact on customs and behaviour. Thus, for example, a nineteenth century married Tripolitan Jewish woman was repeatedly raped by a Muslim state official. Her husband was afraid to complain about the official and in her despair she went secretly to the Jewish court of law to ask for help. The *dayanim*, too, were afraid to take action. When the chief of the Jewish strongmen heard about it, he decided to help her. He planned to hide in the woman's house and confront the rapist when he would arrive. When the *dayanim* heard about this plan, they accused the strongman of impropriety and punished him with a beating. The *dayanim* then met with the Head of the Jews and the strongmen, and the latter managed to trick the official out of his house, beat him, threaten him, and eventually stop his molestation of the woman (Hacohen 1978, 120–121). This case indicates a number of points: it was possible for men in power to molest women while the traditional male protectors of the women were afraid to intervene; the official leaders of the community, too, were afraid to take action; and when the unofficial protector of the community tried to intervene, he was blamed for behaving immorally and was punished for it. Only later did the strongmen manage to find a way to threaten the evil-doer without being in close contact with the woman.

The synagogue and worship

It was not customary for women to take an active role in the service in the synagogue in the format prescribed by men. Women were, however, involved in synagogue life in various other ways. Thus, although the esteemed positions and activities as determined by men excluded women, the latter developed their own ways of participation in manners which might have even been more fulfilling and meaningful for them.

Men and women did not occupy the same space in the synagogue. Moreover, it seems that the synagogue was primarily men's exclusive territory during religious services and study times. Several synagogues in Tripoli, Benghazi, and Khoms had a separate section for women (*'ezrat nashim*) for regular or special occasions. It is not clear whether other small towns and villages included similar special sections. In addition, it seems that the women's section was added when synagogues were renovated or when new ones were built from the nineteenth century on. Thus, at least three synagogues in Tripoli had women's sections: the Great Synagogue (Hacohen 1978, 192), *Dar al-Qa'id*, which was established in 1790 and rebuilt in 1879 with a women's section (Hacohen 1978, 250), and *Dar Barukh,* which was established by a British national from Gibraltar in 1830 and was often frequented by Europeans (Hacohen 1978, 248). In Benghazi, the Great Synagogue (*Sla Kbira*) was rebuilt in 1870 with a balcony which served as a women's section, and through its windows women could see the Torah scroll (Hacohen 1978, 337). Another synagogue in Benghazi was *Slat l'Bramli* which was built in 1840, and had one attic serving as a women's section during *Yamim Nora'im* (High Holidays) (Hacohen 1978, 337). In Khoms, the women's section was at the upper level (Hacohen 1978, 325).

The Jewish community in Libya, like orthodox Jewish communities elsewhere, provided for the education of boys, so that later, as men, they would be able to participate in the synagogue services. One should, however, remember that the reading ability of most Jewish men was very limited, and while they could decipher the words in the Torah and prayer books, they often did not understand their meaning. This resulted from the fact that the sacred texts are in Hebrew and Aramaic while the spoken language was usually a Jewish dialect of the local language, like Judeo-Arabic in Libya. Thus, occupying the honoured space, men attended services in the main auditorium, recited the words of the holy books, and made the appropriate gestures, but more often than not did not understand their own recitations and prayers (Simon 2000, 87–88).

Since it was not expected that women would actively participate in the synagogue service in the same way men did, the community did not provide for their education, and most of them were illiterate. Those women, who chose to participate in the service, though in their special section, were at times ridiculed. Thus, indigenous women, who did not know how to formally pray, used to mock at European Jewish women who attended the services in *Dar Barukh* in Tripoli and prayed from the book (Hacohen 1978, 248–249). This attitude apparently resulted from the fact that the latter followed what was considered to be male behaviour patterns but still remained secluded in the women's section.

Most indigenous women developed their own forms of prayer because most of them could not read and they were denied the right to join in the male-led religious service. They used to stand at the entrance of the synagogue, in the women's section or on nearby roof tops on the Sabbath, the New Moon, and on holidays to watch the Torah being taken out of the Ark (where it is always kept in the synagogue). They would then stretch their hands towards the Torah scroll and ask for the success and health of themselves and their relatives. Sometimes, when the Torah was taken out, they would joyfully ululate loudly in its honour: ru-ru-ru-ru-ru (Hacohen 1978, 192, 248–249, 253–264, 337). Thus, although most women did not follow the prescribed texts and rituals, they understood, meant and felt every word and sound they uttered. Women were also not interested in listening to the public reading of the Scroll of Esther in Purim and preferred to hear it at home (Hacohen 1978, 198), apparently because they could not understand the text. During Yom Kippur girls aged 9–11 used to gather in the vicinity of the Great Synagogue of Tripoli, wearing elegant clothing, playing and singing before the crowd (Hacohen 1978, 192).

Despite the fact that women were not permitted to attend services in the main auditorium of the synagogue and did not fully participate in the male-prescribed services, some women, usually elderly widows, contributed to the establishment of houses of prayer. *Dar Shweika* synagogue in Tripoli was originally the house of a widow named Shweika, of the Guetta family. She endowed her home and in 1816 it became a permanent house of prayer (Hacohen 1978, 248). In another case, Hidriya, the widow of Eliyahu Kahalon, donated 600 francs in 1892 for the establishment of a synagogue in Zliten (Hacohen 1978, 327). These incidents, which were not unique to Libya, show that women valued their involvement in synagogue life, and that widows had a say in the use of their property. Although women funded these synagogues, it was not mentioned whether they included a women's section.

Women also contributed to the proper maintenance of the synagogue. On the eves preceding the Sabbath and holidays, a number of old women would be chosen to clean the floors of the synagogue, rinse the candles, and light them with especially donated olive oil (Hacohen 1978, 254). While cleaning might seem an inferior occupation, touching venerated objects was felt like an act of sanctification, and at times it could also indicate ownership.[4]

Oil donations to the Great Synagogue of Tripoli were regarded as an offering that would be rewarded with good fortune. Even unmarried Muslim women, who had trouble finding a mate, sometimes visited the synagogue on Friday noon with an offering of oil. They would then circle the Holy Ark seven times with a Jewish woman following them with a stick shouting: 'run, fortune is coming! coming! coming!' It was claimed that usually these Muslim maidens would get married within a year, and then donate generously to the synagogue (Hacohen 1978, 254).

Another form of worship was fasting. One fast lasted for six days, in advance of the reading of the weekly portion of the Torah known as *Parashat Mishpatim* (at the end of the Jewish month of Shevat). In this case, many men and women would fast from the end of the Sabbath to the following Friday, namely, Sabbath eve, neither eating nor drinking. It was told that women who were not married yet would often get married within one year of this fast. Some would fast for three days and nights (Hacohen 1978, 199; Tully 1957, 48). On the eve of a new moon, many men and women used to fast and in the afternoon men took out the Torah scroll, dissolving vows and collecting donations. In addition, women used to stretch their hands towards the Torah scroll and ask for the success and health of themselves and their relatives (Hacohen 1978, 253).

Women regarded certain religious objects as having particular healing powers. Thus, the 'yad', or 'hand' (the object used for pointing to the words while reading from the Torah scroll at the synagogue) was used by women to rub the gums of teething babies, believed to ease their pain and stop their crying (Simon 1992, 159). Women also used to borrow the manuscript of *Sefer Migdal 'Oz* when they had difficulties in going into labour. The manuscript was wrapped in a kerchief, brought over to the pregnant woman, and it is said that she usually gave birth after this (Hacohen 1978, 266).

Women's poetry

Most Libyan Jews did not know Hebrew and could not understand Hebrew texts, such as the Torah, prayers, rabbinical literature, and poetry. Most women could not even follow recitations when holding the script, because until the late nineteenth century only few of them could read at all. Contrary to men, who for the most part were passive recipients of literature, women developed their own oral poetry in Judeo-Arabic, their lingua franca. This poetry was understood by all of them, and not only could they follow the poems but also contributed to them as called for by current public and private events. Poems were sung in private or in groups, on various occasions (Simon 2000, 89–90). Thus, rural women used to sing special songs while grinding flour in the early dawn, and as many women might be grinding and singing at the same time, their singing was heard all over the village (Hacohen 1978, 308). This helped distract them from the hard and tedious work. The singing also signalled to the whole community that a woman was indeed awake and fulfilling her duty, thus she could not be insulted as being 'lazy'.

Some poems were related to family events and worship. An important family event was the circumcision ceremony, in preparation for which women known as *zamzamat* had special songs (Hacohen 1978, 272). Other occasions which called for special songs were related to saint veneration, which was common throughout the region amongst both Jews and Muslims. Thus, women composed a song in honour of Sabetai Zvi (the seventeenth century false messiah) and his student, Nathan of Gaza: *Hanun ya rahman, jib al-Mashiah ma'ahu Natan* [the merciful and compassionate brought the Messiah together with Nathan]. Rabbi Abraham Adadi reproached them for it and in 1860 changed the words '*ma'ahu Natan*' with '*Livyatan*' [Leviathan] (Hacohen 1978, 93). The opposition of the male rabbinical authorities to female popular worship did not, however, have much influence on the women's behaviour, and they continued with their unorthodox practices.

Poems recited by women contained at times some historical information. Thus, one poem mentioned a certain Muslim, named Ahmad, who secretly converted to Judaism in 1688 and changed his name to Abraham (Hacohen 1978, 95).

Conclusion

While religion and local custom in Libya had set clear gendered spaces for Jewish men and women, the boundaries were in fact blurred and flexible, especially as one moved further from the centres of authority, Ottoman and Jewish alike. Moreover, economic necessity had also contributed to the widening of women's space. In the village, women often worked outside their homes, with non-kin men around, or even went outside the village, completely unsupervised. This enabled inter-gender contacts, which could end in marriage. Yet once betrothed, the community enforced strong rules of segregation and chastity upon the couple until the wedding. In town, inter-gender contacts were more difficult, yet the community, at least in Tripoli, provided for an annual event in which the youth could observe each other in public and for the men to choose a partner. Poor urban women had to seek waged work and women in general bought merchandize from male peddlers in rural and urban areas. And while the official forms of religious worship excluded women, the latter felt close physical attachment to places and objects of worship. Women developed their own forms of prayer and art which might have been more meaningful to the individual than the more prestigious prescribed rituals men followed.

Notes

1. Unless otherwise stated, this refers to Jewish women in Libya.
2. Hacohen 1978 is a detailed history and ethnography of the Jews of Libya, which was written by Mordecai Hacohen (1856–1929), a learned Libyan Jew from Tripoli, on the basis of his extensive reading of local and European sources as well as his travels in Tripolitania and contacts with its people.
3. Brothels existed in Tripoli and were publicly open, with prostitutes beckoning men to come in. In 1900, the Ottoman governor forbade prostitutes to be seen from the outside, and whoever sought their services had to knock on the door in order to enter. The religious affiliation of the prostitutes is not mentioned. See Hacohen 1978, 171.
4. For example, fights at the Church of the Holy Sepulcher in Jerusalem were over the issue which Christian sects had cleaning rights in certain areas claimed by other sects. See Simon 1985.

Disclosure statement

No potential conflict of interest was reported by the author.

References

Hacohen, Mordecai. 1978. *Higid Mordekhai*. Jerusalem: Ben-Zvi Institute.
Simon, Rachel. 1985. "The Struggle Over the Christian Holy Places During the Ottoman Period." In *Vision and Conflict in the Holy Land*, edited by Richard I. Cohen, 23–44. Jerusalem: Ben-Zvi Institute.
Simon, Rachel. 1992. *Change within Tradition among Jewish Women in Libya*. Seattle: University of Washington.
Simon, Rachel. 1993. "Jewish Itinerant Peddlers in Ottoman Libya: Economic, Social, and Cultural Aspects." In *Decision Making and Change in the Ottoman Empire*, edited by C. E. Farah, 293–304. Kirksville: Thomas Jefferson University Press.
Simon, Rachel. 2000. "Between the Family and the Outside World: Jewish Girls in the Modern Middle East and North Africa." *Jewish Social Studies: History, Culture, and Society* 7 (1): 81–108.
Simon, Rachel. 2001. "Jewish Defense in Libya." *Jewish Political Studies Review* 13: 107–141.
Tully, Miss. 1957. *Letters Written During a Ten Years' Residence at the Court of Tripoli*. London: Arthur Barker Limited.

Finding women and gender in the sources: toward a historical anthropology of Ottoman Tripoli

Nora Lafi

ABSTRACT
This article offers an anthropological reading of Ottoman sources on Libya to shed light on the history of women in Islamic contexts while addressing key issues of gender, power, and representation in history writing. It features the potential of a method that, while illuminating the presence of women in a variety of archival and textual Ottoman sources, questions the gendered nature of their representations as historical subjects. In so doing, the article contributes to current debates on history writing and articulates the perspective of a scholar of Women's History in the Islamic context. The article first outlines some of the challenges that have been identified and tackled by feminist historians over recent decades as for the search for sources in which women's lives can be retraced. It then introduces the main sources that were used in the research – a civic chronicle and a petition – and proposes more general reflections on method in historical research, in which the possibility of tracking women's life journeys in predominantly masculine sources is critically explored. Finally, a series of female figures emerging from such sources as for the case of Ottoman Tripoli (North-Africa) is studied, with an effort of reflection on social typologies and categories in which women were often reduced to clichéd characters like the Wife, the Widow, the Slave, and the Prostitute.

Writing women's history in an Islamic context

This article offers an anthropological reading of Ottoman sources on Libya to shed light on the history of women in Islamic contexts while addressing key issues of gender, power, and representation in history writing. It features the potential of a method that, while illuminating the presence of women in a variety of archival and textual Ottoman sources, questions the gendered nature of their representations as historical subjects. In so doing, the article contributes to current debates on history writing and articulates the perspective of a scholar of Women's History in the Islamic context. I will start by outlining some of the challenges that have been identified and tackled by feminist historians over recent decades, before introducing my sources – a civic chronicle (*yawmiyât*) and a petition (*shakwa*) – and a series of representations of female figures emerging from them: the Wife, the Widow, the Slave, and the Prostitute in Ottoman Tripoli.

Tripoli became part of the Ottoman Empire in 1551, when local notables asked the Empire for protection against Spanish attacks. Between 1711 and 1835, a local dynasty, the Qaramanli, who originated from the Ottoman Anatolian Beylik of Qaraman, ruled the province. The dynasts were early integrated into local society by multiple marriages with local women. In 1835, as a reaction against the risk of colonisation after the French occupation of Ottoman Algeria, Istanbul ousted the dynasty and returned Libya (Tripolitania, Cyrenaica and Fezzan) to direct rule. From the 1850s to the beginning of the twentieth century, the Ottomans enacted an ambitious programme of modernisation in the context of the Tanzimat. The Italians eventually colonised the city and the province in 1911.

The way the history of women can be written has been the topic of numerous debates in the historical profession during the last few decades. From the very beginning, the question of the sources has been at the core of reflections: how to access the reality of the life of persons who were often marginalised in their own societies and who rarely had the occasion to produce documents with a chance of ever being seen by the eyes of historians? As some of the founding scholars in the field of the history of women have illustrated and underlined, such debates on methodology, far from limiting research, have sometimes stimulated it (Bock 1989; Rogers 2004; Dayton and Levenstein 2012; Gabaccia and Maynes 2013; Perrot 2014). But the inertia of representations and perceptions of Middle Eastern and North African societies as particularly patriarchal and as not having generalised as early as elsewhere institutions of female education has preserved strongly gendered dichotomies and restricted the capacity of historians to write a history that could dedicate specific attention to women (Freitag and Schönig 2000; Badran 2016). In a seminal article in which she reflected on the history of her own approach to history writing, Gisela Bock indicated that the existence of strong dichotomies in general representations of women's position in society and role in history constituted one of the major challenges for those who wish to write the history of women (Bock 2010). In the case of women of the Middle East and North Africa, such dichotomies are made even stronger and more persistent by the additional force of orientalist clichés (Alloula 1987; Mehdid 1993; Lewis 1996; Yegenoglu 1998; Schick 1999). As some scholars have argued, it is thus a double challenge for historians to write the history of women of the region (Faroqhi 2002; Keddie 2002; Hasso 2005; Krawietz 2008). Cheryl Johnson and Margaret Strobel (1989) reflected on such difficulties in the very first issue of the *Journal of Women's History*. They have since always remained at the core of reflections on history writing. As Guity Nashat and

Judith Tucker (1999, 1991) stated, the endeavour that pioneer scholars had before them was nothing less than to restore women to history. This intent also motivates the work of scholars from North Africa who, like Leïla Blili Temime (1999), Dalenda Larguèche (2000) in Tunisia and Amal Obeidi (2005) in Libya, dedicated their work to the writing of the history of women. A privileged method of gaining access to information about women has been for scholars to look for sources either produced by women or in which the voices of women, even if mediated through masculine intermediaries, were to be heard. Hence, historians have paid special attention to the few diaries or autobiographies written by women that are available for the region. The problem is that such sources are very limited in terms of the social milieus they represent. A few feminine diaries are available for the Ottoman imperial household (Barzilai-Lumbroso 2009). Outside of this specific area, they are very rare for periods before the twentieth century. Starting at the end of the nineteenth century, new practices of autobiographical feminine writing developed in the bourgeoisie of several cities of the region, from Istanbul to Cairo and from Alexandria to Beirut (Both 2013; Herzog 2014). But their number is limited, as is the social milieu they refer to. To find genuine expressions of feminine feelings and experiences, other historians turned to court records as possible sources of an indirect, but relatively lively, echo of women's voices and lives. Court records, indeed, have proven to be precious documents opening up a renewed understanding of the position of women in society, of their personal and collective strategies, and of the constraints that weighed upon them. In court records, women sometimes 'speak' directly to their judges, and even if historians have learned to be cautious about narratives in which the voices of the weak are recorded in an adverse context, this can constitute a precious source. Amira Sonbol (2003) proposed important methodological reflections on the use of such sources and the prospects they open for women's history. Following early impulses from Haim Gerber (1980) about the Ottoman city of Bursa, from the imperial capital Istanbul (Zilfi 1997) to Anatolia (Peirce 2003) and Palestine (Agmon 1998), or from Tunisia (Largueche 2011) to the Balkans (Doxiadis 2010), many scholars of Ottoman Studies have illustrated the importance of this kind of approach for perceiving decisive elements constitutive of the everyday life of women.

Chronicles and petitions as sources for a gendered historical anthropology of Ottoman Tripoli

Sources other than diaries and court records, however, even if written by men and reflecting in their very form and content strong aspects of the patriarchal nature of society, can be used to access information about women. Beyond the masculine bias, which can also be the object of historical and anthropological reflections, the information about women that is available in such accounts is precious. This article focuses on civic chronicles and petitions and attempts to interpret such sources for the sake of women's history. The main sources under consideration here are the civic chronicle (*yawmiyât*) of the old-regime municipality of Tripoli (Trablus al-Gharb, North Africa, in today's Libya), written by the early- and mid-19th-century secretary (*kâtib*) of the city council (*mashikhat al-bilâd*), Hasan al-Faqih Hasan, published by Mohammad al-Ustâ' and 'Ammar Juhayder (1984 and 2001), and a petition by inhabitants of Tripoli found in the central archives of the Ottoman Empire in Istanbul.[1]

First, if historians use a chronicle, the approach is similar to that tested and promoted by scholars who focus on court records: the aim of the researcher is to track information about women in written documents whose function was originally to record important facts and decisions. The difference in the case of the chronicle is that it pertains to the dimension of everyday life. Unlike court records, which by definition exist only in cases of conflicts, litigations, or dimensions of people's life that were regulated by judicial decisions, chronicles evoke women in more ordinary situations. Historians learned to unearth anthropological aspects of everyday life from court records, beyond the fact that what was recorded was not ordinary. Ordinary aspects are even more visible in chronicles. The civic chronicle acted as a register in which a variety of people and their activities were recorded, conveying a representation of the society of Ottoman Tripoli. Hence, many women are mentioned in the chronicle. Aspects of their daily life, as well as ordinary or extraordinary events that happened to them, are described with great precision. Of course, a chronicle dedicated to the governance of urban public affairs focuses less on private matters and aspects of intimacy than do sources pertaining to the judicial sphere and to family law, where such private affairs were sometimes exposed in front of a judge. Such dimensions, however, are not absent from the chronicle, as they are mirrored in descriptions of ordinary events, like when a woman travels to or from the city, a wedding or a festival is celebrated, or commercial transactions involving public supervision include women as sellers or buyers, and in accounts of troubles, problems, and disruptions of public order (riots, attacks, civil war, crime, prostitution, disease). The civic chronicle was also the civil register for families of notables: births, weddings, and deaths were registered. Women were registered the same way as men, as these examples illustrate: 'The mother of Sâlim al-Tabjî passed away and she was buried at Turbet Shâyib al-'Ayn'.[2] or 'The daughter of Sidî Husine was buried on the 21st of the present month of the year 1248h.'[3] The chronicle also registered people entering or leaving the city. Women were mentioned just like men, for example when on the 16th of the qa'ada month of 1244h. (1829), Abdallah al-Maslamânî travelled with his wife, his sister in law and his children.[4] The chronicle also registered incidents in which a woman was mishandled by her husband in public space.[5] This could be used for future reference in a court audience in case of conflict or divorce. The chronicle was also the memory of the city council and of the milieu of notables. Questions of property, inheritance, and morality had to be written down with precision.

Second, petitions – documents that were at the core of the governance system in the Ottoman Empire – can also be considered precious sources for interpreting the position of women in society. Every subject of the Empire, whatever his or her religion, wealth, or occupation, and every recognised group (confessional community, guild, village assembly, city council) was entitled to petition the Sultan in Istanbul to claim justice and respect for his or her rights (Lafi 2011). All petitions were received by a specific bureau and were the object of administrative and political processing. There were also petitions on intermediate and local levels. In some cases, researchers found petitions written by women or traces of such petitions registered in petition registers (şikâyet defterleri) (Zarinebar-Shar 1997; Zacks and Ben-Bassat 2015). Such documents are of course precious for scholars focusing on gender issues, as they embody the direct expression of women before power. Even in the case of petitions written by men, however, interesting information about women can be retrieved. Various dimensions of women's experiences in society are to be seen in such petitions, such as the values society attributed to women and the behaviours it expected from them.

The petition under study here, for example, mentions women in relation to honour, which reflects their social position. It was written in 1872 by a group of 392 male urban notables from Tripoli in a moment of conflict with Istanbul regarding the municipal reforms. Members of the old-regime municipal council and other notables protested against Istanbul's imposition of a new mayor for the reformed municipality. Members of the group took a petition personally to Istanbul accusing this person of immoral conduct and managed to have him replaced. This process served as a kind of mediation through which the old municipal regime found its place in the modern municipality (Lafi 2002). As the words used in the petition illustrate, public honour and intimacy were strongly linked: the honour of a woman was designated as *Al-'ird*, which is also the word designating her hymen. Attacking the honour of a woman, as the denounced person was supposed to have done, was symbolically the same thing as tearing her hymen (*hataka 'urûd al-nisâ'*).[6] In this case, the petition provides historians an entry to complex dimensions of historical anthropology.

Various feminine figures emerge from the chronicle and the petition: a rich woman who became a benefactor of the old-regime municipality with a founding endowment that gave the institution its seat; wives whose actions were decisive for the careers of their husbands; widows active in labour and business; slaves whose destiny involves complex Mediterranean journeys and identities; and other women against whom the accusation of being prostitutes was sometimes used as a political argument. As Julia Clancy-Smith (2015) suggested in her response piece to the 2014 Toronto workshop organised by Elisabetta Bini and Barbara Spadaro on which the present issue is based, the lives of these women and the social appreciations that were voiced about them are elements to be analyzed to advance in the direction of a gendered history of Libya. To this end, various categories of anthropological analysis can be mobilised. The sources, indeed, occasionally provide information on what constituted the dimension of intimacy for women: their life itineraries, their intimate relationships, their family ties, and their sexuality. On this latter dimension, Leslie Peirce (2009) proposed instruments of interpretation that are very useful when dealing with sources that almost always have a masculine bias. To understand the nature of the intimate universe of women, words used by men about them have to be deciphered and confronted with categories of anthropological analysis. Historians can also look for clues on the distinction, limit, and dimension of in-betweenness between the public and the private spheres. Male sources sometimes make it possible to understand the both hard and subtle definition of such limits (Rizk Khoury 1997). As Elisabeth Thompson (2003) suggested, looking at the various declensions of these categories and articulations of these spheres is key to understanding the experience of women in societies of the region. At the interface between the intimate and the public, various concepts of reputation and honour were decisive in how women interacted with society and how society projected values upon them, their actions, and their bodies. In Ottoman Tripoli, as the sources chosen for this research frequently illustrate, these concepts were also fundamental. They were present here on various levels in the phases of constituting the categories of interpretation. The notion of public morality as analyzed by Abdul-Karim Rafeq (1990) for the case of Ottoman Damascus was also used as a framework for understanding how the position of women in society was the object of complex categorizations and speculations in male sources.

Violence constitutes a central category of this essay in historical anthropology, as a component at least potentially present on various levels in women's lives. Many scholars of gender studies have already underlined the importance of this dimension (Faroqhi 1997; Sonbol 1997; Tucker 2014). Very often, violence was part of masculine actions toward women involving some of the other spheres listed above: mostly intimacy on the domestic level, sexuality, and reputation. Violence was also present in society in general, in the form of wars, riots, repression, and legal penalties. Building on my earlier research on gender and violence against women in Cairo under the Napoleonic occupation, my reading of the sources for this article aims to make some observations on women and violence in Tripoli.[7] Although the sources under examination here do not always directly confront the harshness of these themes, I will try to unearth them when possible.

As for Tripoli, our knowledge of the female condition relies mostly on studies of a specific community, the Jewish one. Very few studies were devoted to women of other communities. The anthropologist Harvey Goldberg (1980) published the civic and communal chronicle of the secretary of the Jewish community of Tripoli in late Ottoman times, Mordechai Akohen. From this research, in a seminal article (Goldberg 1978) on the condition of women in Tripoli, he published important information about and interpretations of the women of the Jewish community, notably their marital status and their involvement in work and artisanal production. Historians like Rachel Simon also specifically focused their research on Jewish women in Tripoli and Libya in general (Simon 1992, 1999 and 2013). The civic chronicle and the petition analyzed here provide more encompassing representations of the lives of urban women in Ottoman times. This study identifies and questions the various categories used to represent women in male sources. My aim as a historian is as much to reveal the content and nature of the category as to interpret its meaning in society and sift through the detritus of masculine representation of women's experience. Hence, the following sections unfold around five main spheres of representations of the feminine in Ottoman Tripoli: the civic sphere, the sphere of family affairs, the sphere of guilds and work, the sphere of slavery, and the sphere of prostitution. Of course, as the previous paragraphs have illustrated, all these spheres were connected, at least in male discourses about and representations of women when, for example, one sphere was evoked in order to weaken a woman's position or that of her family in another sphere.

Women and the urban civic sphere: questions about a municipal endowment

When thinking of North Africa or of the Islamic world in general, the idea of women's participation in public affairs does not seem obvious. The very existence of a local civic sphere has been the object of decades of clichés, speculating on the absence of such a dimension in the cities of the region. It is only recently that scholars have unearthed and acknowledged the existence and consistence of a such sphere: there was in Ottoman cities a dimension of old-regime municipal urban government that was in the hands of the most powerful families of notables, either of noble origin or belonging to the most prestigious guilds or families of merchants. A council of notables had the responsibility to govern many functions pertaining to urban life, like market regulation, building regulation, public order in the streets, public morality, public hospitals, and such public utilities as public fountains, public ovens, and public baths (Lafi 2002 and 2018). People belonging to non-Muslim families, mostly Jewish in the case of North Africa, but also Greek, Coptic, Chaldean, Syriac, and Armenian elsewhere in the Empire, were represented in these institutions by the chief of their community, who was generally a member of the city council. The secretary of the city council was in charge of writing a civic chronicle, whose function was to provide a record of all events and decisions involving the city as a collective body. The Ottoman Empire recognised the existence of these urban institutions from the very beginning of its extension into the Arab world and integrated them in the complex system of governance that was part of its very nature. In the second part of the nineteenth century, this system was modernised during the era of the *tanzimat*, with the creation of modern municipalities based on the old-regime ones (Lafi 2005 and 2006). This fact invited scholars to revise their judgments of the relationship between modernising impulses and local societies. Notions like 'Europeanization' or 'Westernization' were challenged by the evidence of an institutional continuum between old-regime urban institutions and modern municipalities (*belediye*). The prosopography of notables also illustrates this continuum, notables from the old-regime council generally becoming municipal councilors, sometimes after a phase of conflict, as in the case of Tripoli at the time of the petition under study here.

All functions in the city administration, however, were embodied by male notables. A few occurrences of female chiefs are mentioned in the old-regime history of Libya and on several occasions for cities other than Tripoli, for example Morzuk, where a woman is reported to have exercised the functions of *sheikha* in late Ottoman times (Abd al-Qâder 1974; Al-Tawîl 1999), so even if we cannot present the masculine character of the functions as an anthropologically stable feature, the fact is that men were almost always in charge. This was the case in Tripoli, as in all other Ottoman cities throughout the Empire. The general perception in the existing literature is that women entered politics or civic debates only when the season of political modernisation arrived, possibly under European influence, even if in Europe itself women were barred from this sphere sometimes up to the mid-twentieth century (Maksudyan 2014). Of course, if one limits one's perception to active participation in institutions, the absence of women in the governing bodies of Ottoman cities is very true. The sources under examination here, however, provide curious information that invites us to nuance the absolutely gendered dichotomy that dominates perceptions about the history of the old-regime municipal institutions in Tripoli. In this city, indeed, as the chronicle reveals, an important moment in the institutional development of the old-regime municipality was the result of the action of a woman. This suggests a greater degree of women's civic engagement than the simple dichotomy included/excluded implies.

Until the intervention of this woman in the 16th century, at the beginning of the Ottoman era,[8] the municipal council used to gather in the house of its chief, the *sheikh al-bilâd*. The seat of the institution changed every time a new *sheikh al-bilâd* took office. The city hall was de facto the house of the *sheikh al-bilâd*, always an important Muslim notable of the city who owned an important house. There was no stable seat until this woman, mentioned in the chronicle, created a civic endowment (*waqf*) to provide the institution a stable seat (*Baladiyya Tarablus* 1973; Lafi 2002, 149). This woman offered the old-regime municipality a house that became the city hall, first known as *qahwat sheikh al-bilâd* (café of the *sheikh al-bilâd*) and then as the municipal office (*baladiyya*). It was not rare per se that a woman created a *waqf* and that an urban function was constituted in the form of an endowment. Researchers have abundantly illustrated how women could find themselves in the situation of launching or managing *waqf* endowments (Fay 1997; Meriwether 1997). The role of the *waqf* system in urban euergetism, this practice inherited from Hellenistic and Roman times that consisted in urban notables granting their city public amenities in order to reinforce their social and political influence, is also quite common in cities in the Middle East and North Africa. Public fountains, public baths, and public amenities in general were often donated by rich notables of the urban council to the city as a collective body. In the case of old-regime Ottoman Tripoli, too, most public amenities, from fountains to baths and ovens, had been given to the city in the form of a *waqf* constituted by a notable who had dedicated part of his wealth to public service. Once this *waqf* was instituted (and recorded both on site by a graved inscription and *per scriptum* in the civic chronicle), the *mashikhat al-bilâd*, the old-regime municipality, was responsible for its management. Donations generally included money or revenues not only for the construction of the amenity, but also for its management in future times. Part of the sessions of the city council, as the chronicle reveals, were dedicated to the supervision of the urban *waqfs*. Decisions about them were written in the civic chronicle so that later decisions would be informed by the memory of debates about the previous ones. Civic endowments were part of how notable families legitimated their belonging to the circle of urban notability.

What is extraordinary in 16th-century Tripoli is the conjunction of both facts: a feminine and civic *waqf*. The house that was donated was a nice house in the old city in the area of the market called the *Suq al-Turk*, one of the main areas of urban development of the old-regime Ottoman period. This market was the result of a negotiation between the imperial sphere and local notables (who were also the main landowners and merchants of the city). The location of the house illustrates that the old-regime city council was basically a council of merchants. After the donation, all meetings of the council of the *a'yân* took place there. All inhabitants, of all faiths, knew it was the place where decisions on urban regulation were made. As the chronicle illustrates on an almost daily basis, it is where they came with complaints and petitions. This place was dedicated to negotiations and conflict resolution (only serious cases were brought to the justice system of the *qadi*). It is also where the civic chronicle was written and kept. The place became the seat of the modern municipality (*baladiyya*) during the tanzîmât era (1 August 1867, after a phase of transition that began in the mid-1850s). The fact that the civic *waqf* came from a woman was part of urban memories, and the founder of the endowment was remembered as a major city benefactor. There are other cases of civic *waqfs* created by women in other cities of Ottoman North Africa. In Tunis, for example, a woman, Aziza Othmana, founded and funded a new public hospital and other public amenities and charitable organisations during the 1660s.[9] Although her case is specific, as she was a princess of the Muradite dynasty, this, together with cases like the one of the female municipal benefactor of Tripoli, suggests that historians should revise the categories of their perception of the anthropological position of women in society: these women, probably widows, not only had money, but were also entitled to manage it themselves. They also had a civic conscience and had access to the civic sphere, even if they were not members of the civic council.

Being the wife of an urban notable: sociability, motherhood, and reputation

The second aspect the sources under examination here open to is the position of women in the family. Hasan al-Faqih Hasan's chronicle provides numerous indications about the life itineraries of women between marriage, motherhood, and the social role of married women. Wives of notables are of course those whose lives and actions were most intensely followed, due to the importance of their reputation as relatives of their notable fathers, husbands, and sons: it was a duty of the writer of the civic chronicle to report all facts pertaining to such women, from birth to marriage and from inheritance to reputation. The very definition of notability (and thus the family's access to the civic sphere) was at stake. The petition under examination here also provides, negatively, precious indications of social representations attached to women regarding family life, marriage, and their expected behaviour in society. Marriage was the result of complex interactions in the milieu of the notability, and this institution was the receptacle of social representations that went much further than just intimate and family relations: there was a dimension of negotiation between families and factions. Alliances were at stake, as well as the modes of transmission of property and businesses. Scholars have studied this dimension abundantly. In the case of Tripoli, Ben Musa Taysir (1988) explored the life of women at the moment of the negotiation of their marriage. This is also the kind of dimension Colin Imber (1997) studied for the Ottoman Empire in general around the concept of *mahr*, one of the multiples types of dowries. Fatima Guéchi (2000) provided a very precise description of the procedures pertaining to the payment of the dowry in Ottoman Constantine (Algeria). Judith Tucker, studying Ottoman Palestine, has illustrated how family ties were instrumental in defining the identity and social role of women, but also of men. These historians, however, did not focus on chronicles as sources. What the Tripoli chronicle shows is that these matters were of such importance that they were recorded in the civic chronicle: they were constitutive elements of the very definition of the civic sphere. This means that the chronicle served as a proof of payment and of social status. It was possible to refer to it even generations later, either in case of conflict or to prove the reality of a person's belonging to the city's notability. The act of paying the *mahr* (*al-wartha*) was public, certified by a trusted witness who was a member of the municipal council, and was an act of civic value. Hence its recording in the chronicle, for example in the case of the wife of Sî Mahmûd Drîbîka in 1247h. (1832).[10] The procedure of inheritance also involved a repayment of the dowry and was carried out in front of the chief of the city, as in a case from 1243h. (1828) in front of *sheikh al-bilâd* Ahmad Mahsan.[11] If no one could claim to inherit the dowry of a dead woman, the city as a collective body received the inheritance. This is why all details about the dowry were part of the civic chronicle, as a case from 1244h. (1829) illustrates, when a woman named Lalâ Mannanî had her dowry registered in the chronicle.[12] Details were also registered in advance and used when a woman remained widowed, repudiated, divorced, or isolated due to war or exile.[13]

In the chronicle, the recording of weddings in families of notables was always made with mentions of the elements that made the notable a notable: 'During the night of Friday 11 Rabî'I 1229h. (1814), Sîdî Ahmad Bey – may God protect him – married the daughter of Sîdî Ahmad, the chief of the Port (*raïs al-marsâ*).'[14] Women were, in a way, vectors of the transmission of social qualities. Although always defined by the social identity of a man, as women they were crucial elements in the definition of the social identity of men. As the petition illustrates, remarks on the morality of a woman were arguments against her father's or her husband's fitness to be part of the ruling élite.[15] What was at stake was the very quality of the man's notability.

Women at work in the city

Present-day clichés about the exclusion of women from the world of labour in an Islamic context, which themselves abundantly speculate with orientalist clichés (Abisaab 2009), shouldn't prevent historians from studying the consistence of the involvement of women of the past in this highly socialised environment. In all cities of the Ottoman Empire, just like in all its rural regions, most women took part in productive, commercial, and service activities. What was true in the Balkans (Buturovic and Schick 2007) was also true in Anatolia, the Middle East, and North Africa. For colonial North Africa, Julia Clancy-Smith (1999) has illustrated how women took part in labour activities in many fields of artisanal production. For the Ottoman period in this region, too, historians have shown that the feminine element was far from absent in the working sphere. In Ottoman Tunisia, for example, women were creators, producers, and sellers of some of the most renowned potteries (Sekik 2007). In Ottoman Istanbul, their role extended to many segments of productive processes (Zarinebar-Shar 2001). In specific cases, women could also find themselves in situations of managing businesses, shops, and production workshops, as in the case of 18th-century Cairo studied by Mary Ann Fay (1998). As far as Tripoli is concerned, the consensus among historians relates to a remark by Taysir Ben Musa (1988, 43) that rural women from the region were always freer and more active in labour than urban women. This might need to be nuanced, as the sources under study here show that, in Tripoli, women were quite active in productive and commercial activities and not only had the roles of housewives or of servants employed in the palaces of the court or of the most notable families. Clichéd representations imagine women in no other role than concubines of the local dynasts. It is true that some of the most powerful women in the history of Tripoli had this position, like a Jewish concubine of one of the dynasts of the Qaramanli dynasty, whom French Consul Charles Féraud ironically called Queen Esther in his *Annales tripolitaines* (2005, 263; Goldberg 1994). Some of the Black African concubines of the dynasts were also considered powerful women (Féraud 2005). Beyond this dimension, however, which has been the object of picturesque male orientalist speculations, women were present in markets and shops, hospitals and schools (Al-Tawîl 1999). As for trade, women generally worked in family businesses. This included daily interactions with male clients, male business partners, and male public officials. Their situation and the definition of their social status, though, was generally linked to that of a male member of the family. Wife, mother, sister, daughter, widow: in the chronicle, when women are seen in the business or labour sphere, they are often defined in relation to a man. The chronicle, however, allows historians to find precise traces of their activities and to track their life journeys in society. It was not rare that women had responsibilities. In some cases, women could even become managers of the family business, due to the death of a husband, father, or brother. The fact that they became in charge does not appear to be seen as a rarity, surprise, or anomaly in the writing of the chronicle: rather, it seems to be regarded as a fully normal situation. As the chronicle illustrates, this was the case for the early 19th-century female merchant Lila Zohra.[16] This woman ran several businesses in Tripoli and owned several artisanal and commercial facilities, as well as numerous real estate properties. Her intensive presence in meetings that are registered in the chronicle shows that she was one of the most active traders in the city and that she took part in high-level decision-making processes regarding the organisation of trade. The chronicle does not provide details on how she came to run these businesses. But it registers her actions along with those of fellow male merchants (*tujjâr*) as a quite normal situation. In 1245h. (1829), a conflict with other merchants about some of her business activities and the associated conflict resolution procedure managed by the city council show that she was a dynamic member of the city's trade elite and felt at ease negotiating with males about her business.[17] In this case, she was so successful at defending her business that her main opponent, a certain Hajj Slimane Al-Qarbâ', was expelled from the civic sphere and sought refuge, together with his Jewish associate Wald Shabûna, in the home of the British consul in order to be granted consular fiscal protection and to be able to engage in commerce under new conditions. Not all women, however, were as successful as Lila Zohra in defending their businesses in a world that was dominated by males. The petition under study here indeed underlines that women were sometimes more fragile and exposed than other business owners. The petition (a document that was produced a few decades later) denounces the way the *sheikh al-bilâd* al-Qarqani weakened the position of widows who were active in business in order to confiscate such businesses for his own profit.[18] This man allegedly dishonoured a woman and smeared her reputation as a technique to seize the goods and businesses of a widow.

The urban condition of female slaves

In Tripoli, a city whose main function was as a Mediterranean harbour situated at the point of arrival of cross-Saharan routes (Hunwick 1992; Ahmad 1996), slaves were very present in urban society, maybe even more than in other cities of North Africa (Schroeter 1992). John Wright (1996, 1998, 2007) has studied the crucial importance of this commerce for the city. In addition to those from Black Africa in transit to Europe and the Middle-East (Olpak 2006) and sold on local slave markets, slaves of other origins, mostly European prisoners taken in piracy in the Mediterranean Sea, also resided in the city. In Tripoli, a significant portion of the inhabitants were thus slaves, either European or Black Africans. Their statuses were very different, due both to the existence of different categories of slaves in Islamic law and to the complexity of the Mediterranean economy of piracy and labour. As for Tunis, Ismael Montana (2011) has illustrated how Black Africans constituted a social milieu that both retained its cultural specificities and was stigmatised. Similar logics were at play in Tripoli. There were also numerous ex-slaves and their descendants in the cities of the region and in the Ottoman Empire in general. They could have been freed following either their conversion to Islam, the celebration of a public or private festival, a birth or the circumcision of the son of a notable or dignitary, a testamentary disposition, or an evolution of the regulation of the slave market under Ottoman law (Toledano 1998; Bader 1999; Montana 2013). Slaves were also freed as a propitiatory rite when someone died, as in the case of Lala Aïsha, the wife of Yusûf Pasha Qaramanli in 1240h. (1824):

> She was buried on Wednesday in the Mosque of the late Sidi Ahmad Pasha Qaramanli, just in front of the grave of Lala Zeinuba. At least 230 slaves were freed for her. The city entered a period of 7 days of mourning.[19]

In Tripoli, the most famous example is that of a certain Khalil, an ex-slave who married the daughter of the dynast Yusuf Pasha Qaramanlî.[20] In the Ottoman Empire, a significant share of the population of slaves was female (Erdem 2010; Kozma 2010; Zilfi 2010; Akgündüz 2015), and there were numerous women among the enslaved population of Tripoli. Most of them, at least most of those of Black African origin, worked in family houses. The chronicle sometimes gives indications of their existence and lives. Their living conditions depended greatly on the spirit of these families, ranging from violence and sexual exploitation to less violent life itineraries that could also end in marriage and social integration. Some female slaves (in this case called *amma* in the chronicle) were the property of women. Fatima Guéchi (2000) also observed this phenomenon in the case of 18th-century Ottoman Constantine. Various female slaves are mentioned in the chronicle, as items either of inheritance or of dowries. In the case of a divorce, the female slave generally followed the wife, whose dowry she was originally part of. Female slaves are also mentioned in the chronicle on the occasion of their ceremony of liberation, for example during the celebration of a family event in the ruling family. Some *waqfs* were dedicated, sometimes by female notables or princesses, to the process of liberation of slaves and the provision of dowries for female slaves so they could enter the marriage market and achieve complete social integration. But the most emotional story is probably that of a female slave who was sold for exportation after having been falsely accused of being a thief and who managed to join her protest to the petition against *sheikh al-bilâd* Qarqani when she came back:

> She was sold in Tunis to a man who made her a baby girl, who then died. She came back alone to Tripoli and brought her grievance against *sheikh al-bilâd* Qarqani to the imperial authorities, telling her story in detail.[21]

This section of the petition also mentions a demonstration in central Tripoli in the early 1870s against the *sheikh al-bilâd* by slaves who had been saved from being sold for exportation by an imperial Ottoman intervention, but who demanded the return of their children who had been abducted during this episode:

The Sublime Porte had forbidden the commerce of slaves, but it continued. Sheikh al-bilâd Qarqani exported many slaves to faraway countries. When he was not able to sell them, a fact that made him very nervous, these slaves were very happy. They gathered, male and female together, on Government Square, thanking the Sublime Porte for having saved them from Qarqani's ruse and wickedness. They complained and demanded the return of their children, who had been sold. They wrote a petition about this affair.[22]

The female slaves were among the signatories of this petition asking for respect for their right to live with their children. This episode demonstrates that the female slaves had a certain awareness of existing procedures in late Ottoman society and a certain level of agency and organisation.

Prostitution in the city

The sources under study here also allow us to find traces of women's lives in the field of prostitution. This activity in Ottoman Tripoli was simultaneously a well-organised and well-supervised social reality and the object of moral judgments and accusations that could be made against women to attack their honour and that of their family. Historians of Ottoman cities have studied how prostitution was a widely practiced activity and how specific places in cities were dedicated to it, with a relatively high degree of institutional and social tolerance (Sariyannis 2008; Baldwin 2012; Renda 2015). Archives from numerous cities illustrate that prostitution was the object of repression only when it disturbed public order or expanded into streets, buildings, or neighbourhoods whose tranquility and reputation were thereby damaged. As long as this activity remained either discreet or in tolerated places (and under institutional supervision), it was accepted. Court records from numerous cities illustrate this dimension, for example when neighbours complain about the nuisance resulting from prostitution. What was at stake was not the activity itself, but rather that it happened in places and at times it shouldn't have (Semerdjian 2008). The sociology of prostitutes was complex and reflected various life itineraries that could have weakened the position of these women in society: displacement from rural areas, early widowhood, divorce, repudiation, expulsion from a family due to a premarital or extramarital pregnancy, extreme poverty, rape or sexual abuses, belonging to a specific community, or a combination of these factors (Larguèche 1996; Bornstein-Makovetsky 2013). Widows and repudiated women were particularly exposed to becoming prostitutes: they were not protected by a man or a family anymore and could become sexual prey. To avoid this risk, widows often almost immediately married a brother or cousin of the deceased; this was intended as a protection against the risk of remaining isolated and thus subject to harassment, rape, and then prostitution. There were also prostitutes, mostly European, whose identities reflected the cosmopolitan dimension of Ottoman port cities (Fuhrmann 2009). There were also Black African female slaves or ex-slaves who were sexually exploited.

As for Tripoli, Hasan al-Faqih Hasan's civic chronicle provides a lot of information about prostitution. As the chronicle illustrates on numerous occasions, the supervision of prostitution was a responsibility of the *sheikh al-bilâd* and in general of the city council. Prostitutes were registered in the chronicle and their activities were controlled. In some cases, their anonymity was protected, in other cases not. It is not clear whether the old-regime *sheikh al-bilâd* took a commission on prostitution, as they did on many other activities, like the slave trade, the food supply, and grain imports. If they did, it is not clear whether this was considered an abuse of power and moral distortion of their function or a normal practice. What is sure is that, starting in the 1830s, with new policing rules, their physical proximity to prostitutes and women accused of practicing prostitution became less acceptable. Starting in the 1830s, the traditional spirit of toleration and supervision changed with the introduction of new ways of policing the city. This provoked tension, as the *sheikh al-bilâd* was expected to apply new methods of control. His municipal prisons behind his private house and the town hall, in which prostitutes whose activities implied social disturbances were traditionally temporarily jailed, were replaced by a new place with a new police and bureaucracy. In contrast with previous mentions, in which moral judgments were quite absent and in which understatement was the rule, in the chronicle, prostitution tended to be more criminalised and prostitutes began to be called *al-niswan al-fasidât* (corrupted women):

> A decree by our pasha – God save him – under the responsibility of al hajj Ahmed ben Latif sheikh al-bilâd, states that on al-Riba'a Market and all markets it is forbidden to insult the religion […]. The upper floor of the prison (al-zandana al fawqiyya) is now dedicated to corrupted women (al-niswan al-fasidât), and the watchman (shawush) Mahmud Nasr al-Din was appointed to guard and administer these women. Once the key was handed over, they all went to the café with the mayor.[23]

Accusing a woman of prostitution, or a man of having something to do with the prostitution of a woman, could also be wielded as a political instrument. Accusations or allegations attacking the honour of a woman could be used against a certain family to discredit one of its male members. They could also be used against a politician: in the petition for example, the way the *sheikh al-bilâd* al-Qarqani handled prostitution is used as an argument to prove his moral decadence:

> If he heard of a rich and beautiful prostitute, he watched until adulterous men entered her home. Then he assaulted her while she was adorned with various jewelry and jailed her in his own house. At night, he would sleep with her and steal all the goods she had with her: jewels, accessories, and money. He

then threatened to officially accuse her of prostitution with all the consequences for her, so that she could not complain to other authorities.[24]

The petition also accuses Al-Qarqani of attacking the honour of widows, having sex with them, and treating them like prostitutes in order to be able to buy their goods and properties for little money.[25] Widows (*armâl*) who did not have a protector (*awliyâ'*) were specifically attacked by this mayor, whose decadence is targeted by the petition but whose actions also reflect in some way old-regime practices that are challenged at the time of the tanzimat.

Conclusion

The stories of the women mentioned in this article represent only a small portion of the life itineraries of women in Tripoli, of course. They even represent only a small portion of those mentioned in a chronicle whose narration spans decades. Furthermore, many women whose lives were certainly very important never appear in the chronicle or the petition, be it because they belonged to popular classes or because they never experienced a significant incident. What both the chronicle and the petition illustrate, though, is how the role and position of women in society was determined by a number of factors that pertain to the anthropology of gender and social relations, as well as to specific interactions between various spheres like public life, labour, intimacy, and the civic dimension. All the traces and echoes of women's lives found in these sources converge to invite researchers to nuance the inertia of some lasting clichés about women and about societies of the region in general. This invitation does not intend to promote an idealised or irenic vision of women in society: women's lives were often difficult, and the weight of patriarchy, slavery, and social representations was an everyday burden for many of them. The sources show how women were also often confronted with violence or the fear of it. Prostitutes were the most exposed to such violence, and the chronicle narrates how some of them were sometimes found dead. This was the case in 1249h. (1833) for a girl whose name was anonymized in the chronicle ('Bent … , wahda mafsûda', 'the daughter of … , a corrupted girl'). She was found dead one morning, with signs of extreme violence. Her body was mutilated.

> No one knows who killed her. A ring was found in her hands. Her belongings were found around her body.[26]

Yet, my reading of the sources has demonstrated that women were more involved in the civic sphere, public space, and labour than previously thought. What emerges is also a vision in which the social and cultural order, and particularly the position of women in society, was in no way a stable given, but rather the object of constant negotiations. During the old-regime period, the very definition of the civic sphere resulted from the sum of all these negotiations. In that way, this study of the role and position of women in Ottoman Tripoli can also be an invitation to reflect on the functioning of society in general, with values being both imposed and negotiated and identities being both inherited and constantly redefined.

Sources

Hasan al-Faqih Hasan, *al-yawmiyât al-lîbîya, al-juz' al-'awwal, 958h–1248h (1551–1832)*, edited by Mohammad al-Ustâ' and 'Ammar Juhayder, Tripoli, Markaz Jihâd al-Lîbîyya lil-dirâsât al-târîkhiyya, Text and Archives Series, no. 7, 1984, 977 p. and idem, *al-yawmiyât al-lîbîya, al-juz' al-thânî, al-harb al-'ahlîya wa nihâya al-'ahd al-Qaramânlî, 1248–1251h. (1832–1835)*, edited by 'A. Juhayder, Tripoli, Markaz Jihâd al-Lîbîyya lil-dirâsât al-târîkhiyya, Texts and Archives Series, 7–2, 2001, 1211 p.

Başbakanlık Osmanlı Arşivi (BOA) (Central Archives of the Ottoman Empire), Istanbul, D-61-2004. Petition found in the file Irede meclis-mahsu (Trablus al-Gharb).

Baladiyya Tarablus fî miaat 'amm 1870–1970, Tripoli, Sharika Dâr al-Tibâ'at al-Hâdith, 1973, 1099p.

Notes

1. Başbakanlık Osmanlı Arşivi (BOA), Istanbul, D-61-2004. Petition found in the file Irede meclis-mahsu (Trablus al-Gharb)
2. *Yawmiyât,* Vol. II, p. 698, n. 4.
3. *Yawmiyât,* Vol. II, p. 697, n. 1.
4. *Yawmiyât,* Vol. I, p. 410, n. 840.
5. *Yawmiyât,* p. 554, n. 1387.
6. BOA D-61-2004. Petition, section 22.
7. In another piece of research, I proposed a typology of violence in the case of Cairo under the Napoleonic occupation in 1800, from the violence of the army to that of revolting factions, from the violence of repression to that aiming specifically at hurting women's reputations, with sexual violence and rape as tools of political vengeance (Lafi 2015).
8. *Yawmiyât,* p. 216.
9. Archives nationales de Tunisie (ANT), Série historique (SH), Daftar 23-14. daftar bihi mahsûl waqf 'Aziza 'Othmana. 1275h.
10. *Yawmiyât,* p. 550, n. 1371.
11. *Yawmiyât,* p. 358–359, n. 653.
12. *Yawmiyât,* p. 411, n. 845.
13. *Yawmiyât,* p. 124–125, archive n. 51.
14. *Yawmiyât,* p. 234, n.165.
15. BOA D-61-2004. Petition, Section 22.
16. *Yawmiyât,* p. 448–450 n. 961 to 966.
17. *Yawmiyât,* p. 448–450 n. 961 to 967 and 968.
18. BOA D-61-2004. Petition, section 22.

19. *Yawmiyât*, p. 292–293, n. 412.
20. *Yawmiyât,* p. 192, 248, and 290.
21. BOA D-61-2004. Section 21.
22. BOA D-61-2004. Section 21. (Translated by the author, like all quotations from the chronicle and the petition in this article)
23. *Yawmiyât,* p. 578–579, n. 1498–9 Monday 22 zî al-qa'ada 1247h (1831).
24. BOA D-61-2004. Petition, section 16.
25. BOA D-61-2004. Petition, section 22.
26. *Yawmiyât*, vol. II, p. 399, n. 1497.

Disclosure statement

No potential conflict of interest was reported by the author.

References

Abd al-Qâder, Jâmî. 1974. *Min Trablus al-Gharb ilâ Sahrâ al-Kubra*, edited by Mohammad al-Ustâ'. Tripoli: Dâr al-misrâtî.
Abisaab, Malek. 2009. "Arab Women and Work: The Interrelation Between Orientalism and Historiography." *Journal of Women of the Middle East and the Islamic World* 7: 164–198.
Agmon, Iris. 1998. "Women, Class, and Gender: Muslim Jaffa and Haifa at the Turn of the 20th Century." *International Journal of Middle East Studies* 30: 477–500.
Ahmad, Saied. 1996. *Commerce et commerçants dans le Sahara Central: les échanges entre le vilayet de Tripoli et l'Afrique centrale de 1835 à 1911*. Aix-en-Provence: Aix-Marseille University.
Akgündüz, Ahmed. 2015. *Ottoman Harem. The Male and Female Slavery in Islamic Law*. Rotterdam: Islamitische Universiteit.
Alloula, Malek. 1987. *The Colonial Harem*. Manchester: UP.
Al-Tawîl, Mohammad Said. 1999. "Madhâhir Ihtimâm al-dawla al-'uthmaniyya bil-mar'a wa al-tifl fî nihâhayat al-qarn al-tâsi' 'ashir: wilâyat Trablus al-Gharb namûdhajan." *Alfusoul al-Arba'a*: 21–86 and 147–153.
Bader, Raed. 1999. "L'esclavage dans l'Algérie coloniale (1830–1870)." *Revue d'histoire maghrébine* 26: 57–69.
Badran, Rula. 2016. "Taqrîr jalsa al-niqâsh al-'îsh al-mushtarak fî Lîbiya." In *al-'îsh al-mushtarak fî Lîbiya*, edited by Riadh Ben Khalifa, 215–232. Tunis: Presses universitaires.
Baldwin, James E. 2012. "Prostitution, Islamic Law, and Ottoman Societies." *Journal of the Economic and Social History of the Orient* 55: 117–152.
Barzilai-Lumbroso, Ruth. 2009. "Turkish Men and the History of Ottoman Women: Studying the History of the Ottoman Dynasty's Private Sphere through Women's Writings." *Journal of Middle East Women's Studies* 5 (2): 53–82.
Blili Temime, Leïla. 1999. *Histoire de famille. Mariages, répudiations et vie quotidienne à Tunis. 1875–1930*. Tunis: Script.
Bock, Gisela. 1989. "Women's History and Gender History: Aspects of an International Debate." *Gender & History* 1 (1): 7–30.
Bock, Gisela. 2010. "Les dichotomies en histoire des femmes: un défi." *Clio* 32: 53–88.
Bornstein-Makovetsky, Leah. 2013. "Ottoman and Jewish Authorities Facing Issues of Fornication and Adultery: 1700–1900." *International Journal of the Jurisprudence of*

the Family 4. Accessed December 21, 2017. https://papers.ssrn.com/sol3/papers.cfm?abstract_id=2382665.

Both, Marilyn. 2013. "Locating Women's Autobiographical Writing in Colonial Egypt." *Journal of Women's History* 25 (2): 36–60.

Buturovic, Amila, and Cemil Irvin Schick, eds. 2007. *Women in the Ottoman Balkans: Gender, Culture and History*. London: Tauris.

Clancy-Smith, Julia. 1999. "A Woman Without Her Distaff: Gender, Work and Handicraft Production in Colonial North Africa." In *Social History of Women and Gender in the Modern Middle-East*, edited by Margaret Meriwether and Judith Tucker, 25–62. Boulder: Westview Press.

Clancy-Smith, Julia. 2015. "Gendering the History of Libya: Transnational and Feminist Approaches." *Journal of Middle Eastern Women's Studies* 11 (1): 98–103.

Dayton, Cornelia H., and Lisa Levenstein. 2012. "The Big Tent of U.S. Women's and Gender History: A State of the Field." *Journal of American History* 99 (3): 793–817.

Doxiadis, Evdoxios. 2010. "Property and Morality: Women in the Communal Courts of Late Ottoman Greece." *Byzantine and Modern Greek Studies* 34 (1): 61–80.

Erdem, Hakan. 2010. "Magic, Theft and Arson: The Life and Death of Enslaved African Women in Ottoman Izmit." In *Race and Slavery in the Middle East*, edited by Terence Walz and Kenneth Cuno, 125–145. Cairo: American University Press.

Faroqhi, Suraiya. 1997. "Crime, Women and Wealth in the Eighteenth-Century Anatolian Countryside." In *Women in the Ottoman Empire*, edited by Madeline Zilfi, 6–26. Leiden: Brill.

Faroqhi, Suraiya. 2002. *Stories of Ottoman Men and Women*. Istanbul: Eren.

Fay, Mary Ann. 1997. "Women and Waqf: Property, Power and the Domain of Gender in 18th c. Egypt." In *Women in the Ottoman Empire*, edited by Madeline Zilfi, 28–46. Leiden: Brill.

Fay, Mary Ann. 1998. "From Concubines to Capitalists: Women, Property, and Power in Eighteenth-Century Cairo." *Journal of Women's History* 10 (3): 118–140.

Féraud, Laurent Charles. 2005 [1927]. *Les annales tripolitaines*. Saint-Denis: Bouchène.

Freitag, Ulrike, and Hanne Schönig. 2000. "Wise Men Control Wasteful Women: Documents on Customs and Traditions in the Kathīrī State Archives, Say'ūn." *New Arabian Studies* 5: 67–96.

Fuhrmann, Malte. 2009. "Down and out on the Quays of İzmir: "European" Musicians, Innkeepers, and Prostitutes in the Ottoman Port-Cities." *Mediterranean Historical Review* 24 (2): 169–185.

Gabaccia, Donna, and Mary Jo Maynes. 2013. *Gender History Across Epistemologies*. London: Wiley.

Gerber, Haim. 1980. "Social and Economic Position of Women in an Ottoman City, Bursa, 1600–1700." *International Journal of Middle East Studies* 12 (3): 477–500.

Goldberg, Harvey. 1978. "The Jewish Wedding in Tripolitania: a Study in Cultural Sources." *Maghreb Review* 3 (9): 1–6.

Goldberg, Harvey. 1980. *The Book of Mordechai*. Philadelphia: Institute for the Study of Human Issues.

Goldberg, Harvey E. 1994. "Les jeux de Pourim et leurs déclinaisons à Tripoli." *Annales. Histoire, Sciences Sociales* 49 (5): 1183–1195.

Guéchi, Fatima Zohra. 2000. "Le Çadâq à Constantine à la fin du 18e s." In *Histoire des femmes au Maghreb: culture matérielle et vie quotidienne*, edited by Dalenda Larguèche, 115–131. Tunis: Centre de Publication Universitaire.

Hasso, Frances S. 2005. "Problems and Promise in Middle East and North Africa Gender Research." *Feminist Studies* 31 (3): 653–678.

Herzog, Christoph. 2014. "The Urban Experience in Women's Memoirs. Mediha Kayra's World War I Notebook." In *Women and the City, Women in the City*, edited by Nazan Maksudyan, 149–168. Oxford: Berghahn.

Hunwick, J. O. 1992. "Black Slaves in the Mediterranean World." *Slavery and Abolition* 13 (1): 5–38.

Imber, Colin. 1997. "Women, Marriage and Property: *Mahr* in the Behcetü'l-Fetâwâ of Yenişehirli Abbullah." In *Women in the Ottoman Empire*, edited by Madeline Zilfi, 81–103. Leiden: Brill.

Johnson-Odim, Cheryl, and Margaret Strobel. 1989. "Conceptualizing the History of Women in Africa, Asia, Latin America and the Caribbean, and the Middle East." *Journal of Women's History* 1 (1): 31–62.

Keddie, Nikki. 2002. "Women in the Limelight: Some Recent Books on Middle Eastern Women's History." *International Journal of Middle East Studies* 34 (3): 553–573.

Kozma, Liat. 2010. "Black, Enslaved and Hungry: Manumitted Female Slaves in Khedival Egypt." In *Race and Slavery in the Middle East*, edited by Terence Walz and Kenneth Cuno, 197–215. Cairo: American University Press.

Krawietz, Birgit. 2008. "Gender Studies als Herausforderung der Islamwissenschaft." In *Das Unbehagen in der Islamwissenschaft*, edited by Abbas Poya and Maurus Reinkowski, 149–167. Bielefeld: Transcript.

Lafi, Nora. 2002. *Une ville du Maghreb entre ancien régime et réformes ottomanes. Genèse des institutions municipales, Tripoli (1795–1911)*. Paris: L'Harmattan.

Lafi, Nora, ed. 2005. *Municipalités méditerranéennes: les réformes urbaines ottomanes au miroir d'une histoire comparée*. Berlin: K. Schwarz.

Lafi, Nora. 2006. "The Ottoman Municipal Reforms Between Old Regime and Modernity: Towards a New Interpretative Paradigm." In *1st International Eminönü Symposium*, 348–355. Istanbul: Eminönü Belediyesi.

Lafi, Nora. 2011. "Petitions and Accommodating Urban Change in the Ottoman Empire." In *Istanbul as Seen from a Distance: Centre and Provinces in the Ottoman Empire*, edited by Elisabeth Özdalga Sait Özervarlı and Feryal Tansuğ, 73–82. Istanbul: Swedish Research Institute.

Lafi, Nora. 2015. "Mapping and Scaling Urban Violence: The 1800 Insurrection in Cairo." In *Urban Violence in the Middle East. Changing Cityscapes in the Transition from Empire to Nation State*, edited by Ulrike Freitag, Nelida Fuccaro, Claudia Ghrawi, and Nora Lafi, 29–51. Oxford: Berghahn.

Lafi, Nora. 2018. *Esprit Civique et Organisation Citadine dans l'Empire Ottoman*. Leiden: Brill.

Larguèche, Dalenda. 1996. "Confined, Battered and Repudiated: Women in Tunis Since the Eighteenth Century." In *Women, the Family and Divorce Laws in Islamic History*, edited by Amira Sonbol, 259–276. Syracuse, NY: Syracuse UP.

Larguèche, Dalenda. 2000. *Histoire des femmes au Maghreb: culture matérielle et vie quotidienne*. Tunis: Centre de Publication Universitaire.

Largueche, Dalenda. 2011. "Women, Family Affairs, and Justice: Tunisia in the 19th Century." *The History of the Family* 16 (2): 231–244.

Lewis, Reina. 1996. *Gendering Orientalism: Race, Feminity and Representation*. Abingdon: Routledge.

Maksudyan, Nazan. 2014. "This Time Women as Well got Involved in Politics." In *Women and the City, Women in the City*, edited by Nazan Maksudyan, 197–135. Oxford: Berghahn.

Mehdid, Malika. 1993. "A Western Invention of Arab Womanhood: the Oriental Female." In *Women in the Middle East*, edited by Haleh Afshar, 18–58. London: Macmillan.

Meriwether, Margaret. 1997. "Women and Waqf Revisited: the Case of Aleppo (1770–1840)." In *Women in the Ottoman Empire*, edited by Madeline Zilfi, 128–151. Leiden: Brill.
Montana, Ismael. 2011. "Bori Practice among Enslaved West Africans of Ottoman Tunis: Unbelief (*Kufr*) or Another Dimension of the African Diaspora?" *The History of the Family* 16: 152–159.
Montana, Ismael. 2013. *Abolition of Slavery in Ottoman Tunisia*. Gainesville: University Press of Florida.
Nashat, Guity, and Judith Tucker. 1999. *Women in the Middle East and North Africa: Restoring Women to History*. Bloomington: Indiana University Press.
Obeidi, Amal. 2005. 'Tatawwar harakat al-mar'a fî al-mujtama' al-Lîbî [Women's Movement in Libya]." *ESCWA-UN*: 1–17.
Olpak, Mustafa. 2006. *Kenya-Crète-Istanbul: biographie d'une famille d'esclaves*. Paris: Özgül.
Peirce, Leslie. 2003. *Morality Tales: Law and Gender in the Ottoman Court of Aintab*. Berkeley: University of California Press.
Peirce, Leslie. 2009. "Writing Histories of Sexuality in the Middle East." *The American Historical Review* 114 (5): 1325–1339.
Perrot, Michelle. 2014. "Histoire des femmes, histoire du genre." *Travail, genre et sociétés* 31 (1): 29–33.
Rafeq, Abdul-Karim. 1990. "Public Morality in the 18th Century Ottoman Damascus." *Revue du Monde Musulman et de Louisiana Méditerranée* 55 (1): 180–196.
Renda, Kerem. 2015. "The State and the Prostitute: Approaching the History of Sex Work in the Late Ottoman Empire." *Researchgare.net*. doi:10.13140/RG.2.1.1714.0563.
Rizk Khoury, Dina. 1997. "Slippers at the Entrance or Behind Closed Door: Domestic and Public Spaces for Mosuli Women." In *Women in the Ottoman Empire*, edited by Madeline Zilf, 105–126. Leiden: Brill.
Rogers, Rebecca. 2004. "Rencontres, appropriations et zones d'ombre: les étapes d'un dialogue franco-américain sur l'histoire des femmes et du genre." *Revue d'Histoire des Sciences Humaines* 11 (2): 101–126.
Sariyannis, Marinos. 2008. "Prostitution in Ottoman Istanbul, Late Sixteenth – Early Eighteenth Century." *Turcica* 40: 37–65.
Schick, Irvin. 1999. *The Erotic Margin*. London: Verso.
Schroeter, Daniel J. 1992. "Slave Markets and Slavery in Moroccan Urban Society." *Slavery and Abolition* 13 (1): 185–213.
Sekik, Nozha. 2007. *Les potières de Sejnane: des femmes et un savoir-faire*. Tunis: Finzi.
Semerdjian, Elyse. 2008. *Off the Straight Path: Illicit Sex, Law, and Community in the Ottoman Aleppo*. Syracuse, NY: Syracuse University Press.
Simon, Rachel. 1992. *Change Within Tradition Among Jewish Women in Libya*. Seattle: University of Washington Press.
Simon, Rachel. 1999. "Mores and Chores as Determinants of the Status of Jewish Women in Libya." In *From Iberia to Diaspora: Studies in Sephardic History and Culture*, edited by Yedida Kalfon and Norman Stillman, 113–128. Leiden: Brill.
Simon, Rachel. 2013. "Education and Acculturation of Ottoman Jewish Women." In *A Social History of Late Ottoman Women*, edited by Duygu Köksal and Anastasia Falieru, 109–131. Leiden: Brill.
Sonbol, Amira. 1997. "Rape and Law in Ottoman and Modern Egypt." In *Women in the Ottoman Empire*, edited by Madeline Zilfi, 214–230. Leiden: Brill.
Sonbol, Amira. 2003. "Women in Shari'ah Courts: a Historical and Methodological Discussion." *Fordham International Law Journal* 27 (1): 225–253.

Taysir, Ben Musa. 1988. *Al-Mujtama' al-'Arabî al-Lîbiî fîl-'ahd al-'uthmânî dirasa târikhiyya ijtimâ'iyya*. Tripoli: Dâr al-Arabî lil-Kitâb.

Thompson, Elisabeth. 2003. "Public and Private in Middle Eastern Women's History." *Journal of Women's History* 15 (1): 52–69.

Toledano, Ehud. 1998. *Slavery and Abolition in the Ottoman Middle East*. Seattle: University of Washington Press.

Tucker, Judith. 1991. "Ties that Bound: Women and Family in 18th and 19th Century Nablus." In *Women and Middle Eastern History: Shifting Boundaries in Sex and Gender*, edited by Nicki Keddie and Beth Baron, 233–253. New Haven: Yale University Press.

Tucker, Judith. 2014. "She Would Rather Perish: Piracy and Gendered Violence in the Mediterranean." *Journal of Middle Eastern Women's Studies* 10 (3): 8–39.

Wright, John. 1996. "The Mediterranean Middle Passage: the Nineteenth Century Slave Trade Between Tripoli and the Levant." *The Journal of Northern African Studies* 1 (1): 42–58.

Wright, John. 1998. "Murzuk and the Saharan Slave Trade in the 19th Century." *Libyan Studies* 29: 89–96.

Wright, John. 2007. *The Tran-Saharan Slave Trade*. Abingdon: Routledge.

Yegenoglu, Meyda. 1998. *Colonial Fantasies: Towards a Feminist Reading of Orientalism*. Cambridge: Cambridge University Press.

Zacks, Fruma and Yuval Ben-Bassat. 2015. "Women's Visibility in Petitions from Greater Syria during the Late Ottoman Period." *International Journal of Middle East Studies* 47: 765–781.

Zarinebar-Shar, Fariba. 1997. "Ottoman Women and the Tradition of Seeking Justice in the Eighteenth Century." In *Women in the Ottoman Empire*, edited by Madeline Zilfi, 253–263. Leiden: Brill.

Zarinebar-Shar, Fariba. 2001. "The Role of Women in the Urban Economy of Istanbul (1700–1850)." *International Labor and Working Class History* 60: 141–152.

Zilfi, Madeline. 1997. "'We Don't Get Along': Women and Hul Divorce in the Eighteenth Century." In *Women in the Ottoman Empire*, edited by Madeline Zilfi, 264–295. Leiden: Brill.

Zilfi, Madeline. 2010. *Women and Slavery in the Late Ottoman Empire*. New York: Cambridge University Press.

Gender, violence and resistance under Italian rule in Cyrenaica, 1923–1934

Katrina Yeaw

ABSTRACT
Italian rule in Libya was maintained, in large part, through the use of collective violence against the Libyan population in what has been called the bloodiest of colonial wars. Women's participation in this conflict mirrored the gendered division of labour present in pre-colonial society. In both contexts, they played important roles by providing crucial support, for example, feeding and caring for men and children and providing essential military aid to fighters. Women were viewed as a necessary component of the *mujahidin*, whose bravery was beyond reproach. Women were also not immune to the violence inflicted by the colonial state which did not distinguish between 'combatants' and 'non-combatants' on the field of battle but, in fact, specifically targeted women for their value to the resistance. To date, scholars have not addressed the pivotal relationship between gender and violence under Italian colonial rule, which shattered existing forms of social organisation through a variety of policies, most dramatically the use of internment camps. Analysing the effects of systemic violence, this article adds to the current scholarship on women and violence during the colonial period in the Middle East and North Africa by drawing on previously published oral history narratives and Italian archival sources to examine the experiences of women involved in the resistance to Italian occupation in Cyrenaica, Eastern Libya, between 1923 and 1934. Ultimately, I argue that women of the region made the rebellion against the Italian occupation possible through their military service by participating as members of extended families and clans.

Introduction

In September 1911, Italy invaded the Ottoman-controlled coastal regions of Tripolitania and Cyrenaica. A relative latecomer to the 'scramble for Africa', Italy aimed to establish colonial possessions in the Southern Mediterranean to compete with other imperial powers, primarily France and Britain (Anderson 1991, 229). However, the Italian government met unexpected local resistance, partially backed by the Ottoman government, preventing it from winning a decisive victory and gaining hegemonic control over the region during the 1910s. By the 1920s, Italy would try to 'pacify' the Libyan population through large-scale military operations and other forms of coercive power and violence. Finally, in 1934, the Libyan resistance was declared defeated, ending a conflict that had started more than two decades earlier (Labanca 2012).

However, the suppression of the armed resistance came at a terrible price for the people of Libya, in general, and of Cyrenaica more specifically.[1] Between 20% and 50% of the Libyan population perished or fled during the occupation, with some estimates claiming the population declined from approximately 1.5 million to 750,000 during this period. Under the leadership of General Rodolfo Graziani, the violence of the Italian occupation was most extreme in the region of Cyrenaica in eastern Libya, the conquest of which has been described as one of the bloodiest colonial wars. To break the resistance, Graziani utilised a policy of total war which included the construction of a four-meter-thick 300-kilometre fence along the Libyan-Egyptian border in an attempt to cut Libyan fighters off from their supply lines into Egypt (Salerno 1979; Guerri 1998, 229; Atkinson 2003, 14; Cresti 2011, 83–104; Labanca 2012, 174–206). When this proved ineffective, he confined the local population in concentration camps to deprive the resistance of its support and aid (Cresti 2011, 97–100).

Analysing the effects of this systemic violence, this research adds to the current scholarship on women during the colonial period in the Middle East and North Africa by drawing on oral history interviews to examine the experiences of women who were involved in the resistance to Italian occupation in eastern Libya. Specifically, it assesses the role played by women in the armed resistance by focussing on aspects of the gendered division of labour within resistance groups. It argues that women in Libya made the long rebellion feasible through critical military duties and participated as members of households and clans and in accordance with local allegiances and religious identities. In effect, I demonstrate how women not only interacted with colonial rule but also shaped its configurations. In addition to the pivotal role of women in anti-colonial struggles, colonial violence was gendered. Like many Mediterranean societies, Libya and Italy shared fundamental patriarchal values when it comes to violence and honour. Men were expected to take responsibility for female kin while elders were required to protect those younger members of the community. Whether through tribal vengeance or duelling, injuries inflicted against kin in both societies required retaliation through violence to avenge the wrong and protect an individual's honour (Chapelle 1958, 323; Hughes 2007). Therefore, violence perpetrated against another's female kin was viewed as a way of humiliating that individual by undermining his honour and manliness. The Italians routinely employed this kind of gendered violence in an attempt to weaken the resistance.

The history of the Libyan resistance and its eventual defeat at the hands of the Italian government still tends to focus on questions of nationalism, state-building and Libyan identity while neglecting issues related to subjectivity, local identities and understandings as well as lived experiences under colonialism. Women are usually at the margins of nationalist and colonial narratives of history; however, here they emerge as central figures as this study addresses the experiences of subaltern members of Libyan society – women, both nomadic and semi-nomadic people – whose stories are rarely recorded and preserved. These voices broaden our understanding of colonialism by challenging accepted narratives about the ways in which it operated at the local level., which raises questions of the shaping of memories and representations of Libyan women, gender, and colonial violence. This marginalisation is reproduced through the silences and omissions apparent in the interviews gathered by the Libyan Studies Center in Tripoli, a nationalist enterprise sanctioned by Qadaffi the new leader of independent Libya, that form the basis of this study, as women are forced to negotiate with the largely masculine narratives of Libyan history.

This article draws on a collection of oral history interviews gathered by the Libyan Studies Center in Tripoli. Starting in the 1970s, the centre began collecting interviews with former *mujāhidīn* and their relatives (Vansina 1994, 175–82). The centre published a collection of these oral narratives in forty volumes under the title of *Mawsūʿat riwāyāt al-jihād (Oral Narratives of the Jihād)*, but a large percent of the 15,000 narratives still remain un-transcribed (Sāʿidī 1983-). Despite the large number of interviews, only a small percentage of them were conducted with women. The majority of the sources drawn upon for this study are edited interviews with male and female resistance fighters published as part of the *Mawsūʿat riwāyāt al-jihād* series. These interviews were all conducted in the Libyan dialect during the late 1970s and early 1980s in eastern Libya, although a few were later transcribed into Modern Standard Arabic. All of the translation in this article are my own unless otherwise noted.

The Libyan Studies Center was a major historical project of the regime of Muammar el Qaddafi. After coming to power in 1969, Qaddafi utilised the new state oil revenue to reframe the history of Libya to fit his own intellectual orientation. In particular, he highlighted the revolutionary role of the people in the creation of the Libyan nation and downplayed regional differences, a position consistent with his own revolutionary ideology (Baldinetti 2010, 21). This new narrative valorised the resistance of the largely male *mujāhidīn* and championed the figure of ʿUmar al-Mukhtār, leader of the resistance in Cyrenaica. The male revolutionary was thus placed at the centre of the construction of a national Libyan history. This version of Libyan history was sanctioned by the authoritarian nature of the new regime that sought to monopolise the official narratives of Libyan history. One keen way of controlling the historical narrative was through negotiations with historians, most notably Jan Vansina, a central figure in the fields of African and oral history, who organised the Libyan collection of oral history narratives in the 1970s. After the fall of the Qaddafi regime, the future of the Libyan Studies Center remains unclear, a reflection of the precarious trajectories of memory and history writing in Libya.

While I have drawn on Italian archival sources to supplement the oral history interviews gathered in Libya, the vast majority of the Italian sources from this period remain inaccessible to researchers, especially military documents accessed from the Ufficio Storico dello Stato Maggiore dell'Esercito (USSME). The available written documents on the 'pacification' of Libya highlight the extreme violence of Italian colonial rule, including the use of chemical weapons and concentration camps, but it is impossible to verify every accusation made in the oral history interviews. Until the Italians open their entire archive to researchers, I only have access to the women's versions of colonial history. While this is not without its limitations, I follow an approach to oral histories developed by Italian historian Alessandro Portelli, who argues that oral history is a method of exploring new areas of events from the perspective of non-hegemonic classes. The strength of oral history lies in the fact that 'it tells us less about *events* than about their *meaning*' (Portelli 2003, 36). While this research evaluates the roles of women in the anticolonial resistance, it captures the way in which they constructed an understanding of colonial rule through an evaluation of their memories of the period.

The social world of the tribes of Cyrenaica

Cyrenaica (*Barqa*) differed substantially from western Libya due to the 403 miles of desert that separated it from Tripolitania. This geographic separation enabled it to develop its own distinct regional culture (Ahmida 2009, 73). This section combines early scholarship on tribes by Emrys L. Peters, Roy G. Behnke and Lila Abu-Lughod and ethnographic evidence drawn from the oral sources to construct the social world of tribes in Cyrenaica.

Bedouin gender ideology is based on the twinned concepts of honour, associated with men, and modesty, associated with women. Within this framework, 'maleness is associated with autonomy and femaleness with dependence' (Abu-Lughod 1986, 118). Along with dependence, women are also associated with nature and natural processes that include menstruation, procreation, and sexuality in a perspective that presents them as morally inferior, since they lack both reason and self-mastery (124).

In practice, women in pastoral societies in Cyrenaica enjoyed high domestic status and the *hijab* was worn only situationally, but women were generally excluded from the company of men in public. A woman wore silk head coverings that were drawn across her face at the approach of a man who was not a close relation (Peters 1990, 247). After the onset of puberty but prior to marriage was the period during which both sexes were the most tightly controlled and were, correspondingly, denied the full rights of married members of the community. Premarital indiscretions were also dealt with harshly and may have resulted in the deaths of both parties involved (247). However, both men and women gained more freedom upon marriage, after which they were seen as making the transition to full adulthood, which usually took place in the mid-teens for girls and early twenties for young men, although this could be delayed considerably to hold out for a high brideprice. Women gained additional freedom as they aged and passed the period of childbearing, no longer covering their faces and conversing freely with men (261).

According to interviews with men and women who participated in the anti-colonial resistance, both men and women were actively involved in the tasks of production, although each had their distinctive roles. Men's tasks included herding livestock, plowing fields, harvesting crops, and storing grain. In contrast, women were involved with the tasks of spinning wool, grinding flour from wheat or barley, fetching water, chopping firewood, cooking, milking animals and weaving carpets (and tents among nomadic and semi-nomadic tribes) (Zahrā 1995, 34). The mixing of gendered responsibilities or cooperation in tasks between men and women was reduced to a minimum. In fact, the interference of men in women's tasks was greatly discouraged. Peters maintained that this helped create a symbiotic relationship between the sexes, since each was dependent on the other (Peters 1990, 250).

Beyond the domestic sphere, women's status also played a part in politics, where marriage alliances were crucial. However, women (and men) had no direct say in their choice of spouse, as marriages were arranged by senior members of the household (Peters 1990, 243). Women in the narratives routinely mentioned their lack of input into choosing a husband and marriage alliances within a single family were common, especially marriage between first cousins (Zahrā 1995, 202–203). Despite being Sunni Muslims, the most common form of marriage was a 'gift' ('*ata*') marriage in which a guardian gives a woman in marriage as if she was not privy to the marriage contract and also claims her dowry (Layish 1998, 4). This practice is not recognised by the four Sunni schools of Islamic jurisprudence, which each recognise the dowry as the woman's property (Tucker 2008, 41–50). Among nomadic tribes of Libya, women's lack of control over her dowry extended to other types of property, since a woman was supported by her father's estate until marriage but did not inherit, either as a wife or daughter. Behnke quoted individuals saying that 'women want husbands not property' (1980, 117). As a result, women owned substantially less property than men, usually consisting of jewellry and other items of personal adornment, which were often part of the bride price (*mahr*).² This relative lack of access to property enshrined the dependent status of women within Muslim Bedouin communities.

While there is some information available about the differences between the social relations of the semi-sedentary tribes of the *al-Jabal al-Akhḍar* and their fully nomadic brethren, especially relating to marriage, it is difficult to ascertain to what extent the semi-sedentary tribes adopted the practices of more sedentary people. It is clear that the tribes of *al-Jabal al-Akhḍar* retained their tribal affiliations and continued to maintain other aspects of pastoral cereal cultivation and forms of animal husbandry. However, evidence suggest they also adopted more orthodox Muslim practices, referring to themselves as '*ahl al-sunna*' (Zahrā 1995, 78), and engaging in stricter segregation of the sexes than was practiced by fully nomadic peoples (69).

This study looks at decades of changes that were intensified by colonial war and violence. These changes altered the social world of the tribes, resulting in previously semi-sedentary tribes becoming completely nomadic during the war. Jamīla Saʿīd Sulaymān, who was born in 1900 in Shahhat (Cirene) in *al-Jabal al-Akhḍar* and participated in the anti-colonial resistance, recounted that the war destroyed grain cultivation and herding and that 'it was not possible to remain in one place' (al-Hāyn 1989, 9).³ During the war, there was also a breakdown in stricter forms of gender segregation (Zahrā 1995, 69).

The women's resistance to Italian colonialism

The interviews and other sources make it clear that some women were an active part of the resistance from the beginning. Their names are often listed among those 'martyred' in various battles, for example, women like Mubrūka al-Qabṭān and Maryam Saʿd al-Khashabī who died in battle in a place called al-Naḍīd (al-Hāyn 1989, 127).⁴ However, not all Libyan women experienced Italian colonialism the same way; rather, their experiences depended on age, status, religion, language, ethnicity, and tribal affiliation. Those women who fought in the anti-colonial resistance were largely from rural tribal backgrounds. Even among those from rural areas, some women stayed with their families and did not participate in the *jihād* (Zahrā 1995, 109). There was no universal feminine experience of the colonial conquest, just as there was no universal male experience.

While there is little source information available about how women joined the *mujahidin*, it is clear from their narratives that all of the women had other family members involved, whether husbands, brothers, mothers or fathers. Jamīla Saʿīd Sulaymān and her 'family joined the ranks of the *mujāhidīn* answering the call of *jihād* in the path of God' when she was a young girl (al-Hāyn 1989, 9). It is unlikely that women (or men for that matter) were recruited en masse as individuals; rather, they joined the resistance along with members of their clan or camp. Tribes in Cyrenaica were divided into smaller sub-groups or camps composed of related males and made up of between 200 and 700 adults (Peters 1990, 60). Members of each camp share a collective identity that requires every member to exact vengeance, pay blood money (*diya*), and engage in common defense of the camp as a whole (61). During the colonial period, it was this tribal organisation that gave the anti-colonial resistance its form, and it was likely this organisation that led women to join the resistance.

As members of tribal groups, women played a pivotal role in the resistance. While women rarely carried weapons, they rode camels loaded with baggage and children, cared for the injured, distributed water, and carried the fallen away from the battlefield (Zahrā 1995, 34). Jamīla Saʿīd Sulaymān confirmed that the 'women helped the wounded and cooked and administered first aid' to the fighters (al-Hāyn 1989, 10). Similarly, al-Sabir Muḥammad Yūsuf al-Tabalqī, who was born in the city of Deriana in northern Cyrenaica in 1913 (al-Barghathī 1990, 7–31), said that 'women participated with us in the battle of al-Qarun by fetching water and distributing it among the fighters while uplifting the morale of the *mujāhidīn* with *zaghārīd* ... which inspired a fighting spirit and inflamed the feelings of the *mujāhidīn*' (23).[5] These interviews illuminate the patterns and circumstances of women's involvement with resistance and colonial violence. Yet, the interview with this *mujāhid* also points to a gendered construction of women as primarily supporting, uplifting, and inflaming figures for the male *mujāhidīn,* rather than being central figures in their own right. This construction has often resulted in downplaying the importance of women's logistical and tactical roles resisting colonial rule.

The tactical and logistical support provided by women were extensions of their responsibilities during periods of greater stability. War is not exempted from the social world, but must instead be understood in reference to its specific social context; sometimes it rejects past traditions while at other times it reproduces and strengthens the former social order (Richards and Helander 2005). All of the women's accounts point to the fact that the gendered divisions of labour which were part of the social organisations of pastoral societies continued during the war against the Italians. Providing water for the fighters, cooking, and caring for the wounded were related to the tasks of fetching water, chopping firewood, cooking that women were responsible for in Bedouin communities. Women's roles were crucial to the maintenance of everyday life in the tribe before the Italian invasion and their roles remained crucial to everyday life of the tribe during war and critical to the continuation of the resistance.

Women were held in high esteem for their bravery, strength, and fortitude and were considered members of the *mujāhidīn* like men. At times, the extraordinary situation of the ongoing anti-colonial resistance enabled women to gain more autonomy on the battlefield than they would have traditionally within their own communities. Mabrūka Yūnis Būqafīfa's father expressed this sentiment forcefully, telling her 'you are a man in my eyes. I have no sons so you are my son' (al-Hāyn 1989, 133), and revealing his high degree of respect for her capabilities by entrusting her to look after the other women as long as she remained alive, a great compliment in a society in which female dependence and male guardianship were the norm (133).

Despite several mentions of women's great bravery, there is only one reference in the narratives to a woman taking up arms against the Italians. One *mujāhid* tells of a woman named Mabrūka al-ʿAmīsha who he saw firing upon the Italians at the battle of al-Halīqīma, but little else was said about her. Although women did not usually take up arms, this did not mean that they were not put in harm's way. As previously noted, the names of woman are listed among those remembered to have died at various battles, for example, Mubrūka al-Qabṭān and Maryam Saʿd al-Khashabī (al-Hāyn 1989, 127). Also, Jamīla Saʿīd Sulaymān recounted the battle of Wādī al-Shabriq wa al-Muhaja in which 'many men and women, old and young', died 'especially those on foot' (al-Hāyn 1989, 10). During the battle, the *mujāhidīn* were split into two groups, one attacking the Italians and one defending their own caravan. Her husband was among those trying to defend the caravan while she ran from the Italians on foot. She recalled that:

> My husband ordered me to ride behind him but I was afraid that he would fall from the horse if he carried me so I refused. I was carrying my infant son on my back and he had stopped crying and moving and I knew for certain he was dead so I cried out my husband to inform him of this ... the child had been wounded by shrapnel during the battle and was dying of thirst before his death (al-Hāyn 1989, 10).

From the horror of the scene that she describes, women (and children) did not escape battle but were often in the midst of it. A number of women tell of carrying small children on their backs in hope of keeping them safe or of watching them and other family members die or be taken prisoner by the Italians.

Nowhere in the accounts do any of the women express any equivocation about the role of the Italians or their motivations, or any of the nostalgia sometimes expressed about the colonial period. In the women's versions of the colonial period, the Italians were always vicious and brutal and the *mujāhidīn* were always brave and heroic. This is probably a result of both the individual experiences of women during the colonial period and the official anti-imperialist ideology fostered by the regime of Muammar el Gaddafi (Baldinetti 2010, 39). The Italians remained shadowy figures, often referred to simply as 'the Christians' (*al-naṣārā*). Khuzna ʿAbd al-Salām al-Kuzza, born in Suluq in 1891, stated that 'no one is afraid of them ... we are girls and the only thing we fear is shame (*al-ʿaīb*)' (Zahrā 1995, 52). Here she invokes a gendered understanding of fear in which dishonour, most likely defined by sexual impropriety, is a greater threat than other forms of bodily harm that the Italians could inflict. This fear of dishonour may have pushed many women into silence in their accounts on the topic of sexual violence and to fashion instead heroic accounts more attuned to male *mujāhidīn* narratives and to their gendered code of honour.

While it can be assumed that those opposing Italian rule ultimately hoped to push the Italians out of the Libyan territories, women explained their involvement as a desire to answer 'the call of *jihād* in the path of God' (al-Hāyn 1989, 9). They also often spoke of the sense of solidarity between the *mujāhidīn*: Hūayna Muḥammad Ibrīdān al-Baraʿṣī said that 'our tent was their tent, our food was one, our drink was one, and our travel one; we were comrades' (Zahrā 1995, 87).[6] Similar to their male counterparts, women did not express any sentiments that could be construed as nationalist or even proto-nationalist about the establishment of a Libyan nation. This is not surprising given the fact that Libyan nationalism did not develop until the second decade of the twentieth century with the collapse of the Ottoman Empire in 1922 and subsequent abolition of the Caliphate (Anderson 1991; Bernini 1999; Ahmida 2009; Baldinetti 2010, 12). Nationalism had a stronger resonance among urban middle-class elites and took significantly longer to filter down to the popular classes. Although the women in this study actively opposed the Italians well into the 1930s, Islam and allegiance to their family and tribe were the two greatest motivating factors in this struggle, rather the ideal of a Libyan nation as such.

The gendered violence of the colonial encounter

A large number of Libyans were killed, exiled, and imprisoned for opposition to the Italian occupation during the first decade of their rule. The Italians were unsuccessful in gaining control of the majority of the territory and the resistance of the local population had pushed them back to the cities of Tripoli, Homs and the coastal strip between Zanzur and Zuara in Tripolitania and the cities of Benghazi, Shahhat (Cirene), Derna and Tubruq in Cyrenaica by 1915. Local notables formed a semi-autonomous government, the Tripolitanian Republic (*al-Jumhūriyya al-Ṭarābulusiyya*), in Tripolitania and the Italian government recognised the control of the *Sanūsiyya*, a revivalist Sufi religious movement, over the hinterland in Cyrenaica and their leader, Idrīs al-Mahdī al-Sanūsī, was granted the largely ceremonial title of Amir of Cyrenaica.[7]

A shift in policy occurred after the Fascist government came to power in 1922, as Benito Mussolini rejected the Liberal government's policy, in place since 1911, of collaborating with local Libyan elites. Mussolini's first Minister of Colonies, Luigi Federzoni, pushed for what the Italians considered the *riconquista* of the hinterland in early 1923 to transform it into a space open for Italian demographic colonialism (Cresti 2011, 92). This *riconquista* was undertaken by Rodolfo Graziani, nicknamed the 'Butcher Graziani' by the local population, who was in command of all Italian forces in Tripolitania by 1928 (288). In 1930, he was appointed the vice-governor of Cyrenaica and instituted a repressive campaign against the indigenous population, which included the clearing of ground, the razing of enemy villages, the seizure of crops and livestock, and destruction of wells. Although Graziani was not solely responsible for the repression of the anti-colonial resistance, he became a symbol for the local population of the tyranny and barbarism of Italian colonial rule. Viewing Libya as Italy's rightful possession, he argued that 'the wheel of fate' had been 'planted and stuck ... a thousand fiery Italian souls' in the 'untouched sands' of the Libyan desert.[8]

Franz Fanon has argued that the first colonial encounter 'was colored by violence and their cohabitation – or rather the exploitation of the colonized by the colonizer – continued at the point of the bayonet and under cannon fire' (Fanon 2004, 1). This kind of systemic colonial violence was experienced by women as well as men. Violence was indiscriminately inflicted on Libyans as colonial subjects, but it was also gendered. Women's experiences of violence overlapped men's but was not identical. There were gendered divides in the way Italians approached men and women involved in the resistance, often using women as ammunition against men. The Italian military consistently inflicted humiliation on Libyan men by attacking women and children in hopes of bringing the resistance to an end by targeting their honour and manhood.

Women were often on foot during engagements and those who rode camels or horses were usually weighed down with luggage and children. Men, on the other hand, rode on horseback unburdened, giving them greater speed and mobility in battle. The Italians did not hesitate to exploit the more vulnerable position of women. The safety of children on the ground during battles was a constant concern for women, with Jamīla Saʿīd Sulaymān mentioning that children 'lived a life of exhaustion and hardship during the war and most of them died during Italian bombardments' (al-Hāyn 1989, 11). The lack of mobility of women and children made them easy targets for capture. For example, at the battle of al-Ḥaqīfât, in the region of Suluq, the Italians captured more than 60 women and imprisoned them at the prison called Giardina (Zahrā 1995, 35). Mabrūka bint ʿAbd al-Raḥmān bin Salīm told of an incident in which her tribe was bombarded by the Italians and the men fled to a nearby area while the women remained. When the Italians arrived, they demanded the women send an agent to the men and broker an exchange between them – their weapons for the release of the women. As a result, the men sent their weapons to the Italians and the Italians let the women go (al-Hāyn 1989, 131).[9] This was not the only case of women being captured by the Italians. In fact, the majority of the women involved in the resistance were captured at least once.

Many women were questioned while in Italian custody. Jamīla Saʿīda Sulaymān, for example, proudly recounts that she stood up under interrogation when the Italians suspected her of being responsible for the downing of one of their planes:

> I was interrogated harshly about the crash of the airplane and I denied that there was any close relationship between myself and the individual who brought it down. I said only that those who were fighting the Italians on that day were from my tribe (al-Hāyn 1989, 12).

And Huniyya Sulaymān Idrīs Abū Baqusa was subjected to more than one interrogation and described the torture of her and her mother at the hands of the Italians:

> They questioned everyone individually and the questions revolved around the *mujāhid* Sulayman Idrīs and our ties with Massʿūd al-ʿUbaydī and if he was the one that had brought that use to the territory of the ʿUbaydāt tribe and if he had helped us in our ordeal. We denied any knowledge of Massʿūd al-ʿUbaydī as he denied any knowledge of us. Both he and his children were tortured because of this. He was thrown to the ground every day and whipped and we suffered the same treatment and were tortured despite our young ages. I remember that among the methods of torture was imprisonment in an enclosed space for seven days without food or water. And they would take my mother out every day and whip her 50 lashes with a whip that was frayed at the end. But she did not respond or reveal the location of my father or the *mujāhidīn* and denied any knowledge of Masʿūd al-ʿUbaydī ... This brutality caused my brothers Ibrāhīm, Abd al-Laṭīf and Ṣalāḥ to flee while my mother failed in an attempt to escape where she was exposed to torture, as I have mentioned, and us little children were the reason for her continued imprisonment. We all suffered under the worst that a person could be exposed to who has fallen into the hands of oppressive imperialists like the Fascist Italian colonizers ... As for my mother, she was tortured continuously for several days and they rubbed salt in the wounds so that it would be more painful (al-Hāyn 1989, 110).

Huniyya Idrīs Abū Baqūsa was young when she witnessed her mother beaten and tortured and was tortured herself. In hopes of extracting information about the location of the *mujāhidīn* and its leadership from them, the Italians subjected the women to extreme physical abuse. Torture was used consistently by the Italian government as a tool to pacify the indigenous population of Libya. In spite of the overwhelming brutality of Italian rule, the employment of torture was not unique to their colonial policies. Torture was intrinsically linked to colonial history and the repressive nature of the colonial state (Lazreg 2008, 3). Pierre Vidal-Naquet, a historian of Algeria, argued that 'the essential feature of the practice of torture ... is that one man or one class of a society claims absolute power over another man or another class of society' (Vidal-Naquet 1963, 167). In the case of Libya, male colonial officers inflicted absolute power over female bodies, which they starved, exposed, and brutalised (Lazreg 2008, 3).

Beyond torture, the capture and confinement of women by the Italians opened them up to a whole range of physical dangers including the possibility of sexual abuse. While the interviews contain references to most extreme forms of barbarism by the Italians, including cutting fetuses from the bodies of pregnant women, accusations of rape or other forms of sexual violence are rare but not completely absent. Many women, including Fāṭima Muḥammad Būnajī al-Masārī, denied outright that Italians raped women and claimed that her sister was captured and held by the Italians but she was returned unmolested. When she was married to ʿUmar al-Mukhtār, he verified her sisters' virginity. The fact that her sister escaped unharmed from Italian custody does not mean that other women did not experience sexual violence, whether that violence was systematic or unorganised. ʿUmar al-Mukhtār may simply have chosen to protect his new wife's modesty before the community and concealed the fact that she was assaulted in Italian custody. Women silencing experiences of sexual violence helped preserve narratives of male honour and female modesty.

In contrast, Ruqiyya al-Fakhrī claimed the Italians regularly took women and girls by force. The forced abduction of women epitomised the relationship between power, gender and ethnicity under Italian rule, under which colonial men could physically claim the bodies of colonised women with impunity. In one case, some Italians came to a girl's father and demanded her, but her father refused since they 'did not betroth women to Christians'. The next day the Italians returned with soldiers and took the daughter away in a car. After he was done with her, he passed her along to an Arab soldier in the Italian military (Zahrā 1995, 109). Those references to rape which do exist in the narratives contain the consistent details of women being kidnapped by Italian soldiers and forced into marriage or concubinage and then passed between men as concubines or sex slaves. Given the silences and shame that exist around this subject, and the emphasis Arab society places on women's chastity as a marker of male honour, Ruqiyya al-Fakhrī is one of the few individuals who directly discusses the rape of Libyan women, including her own kidnapping and rape in Siwa.

Beyond the capture of women, narrators highlight other ways that women and children could be used to punish *mujāhidīn*. The children of *mujāhidīn* were sometimes kidnapped and raised by Italians as punishment for their parents' resistance (al-Hāyn 1989, 14). The Italians also executed the wives and children of *mujāhidīn* who refused to surrender. When Ibrīk al-Lawāṭī, fled to Egypt to avoid capture by the Italian authorities, they executed his wife and daughter in al-ʿAqīla concentration camp as a kind of collective punishment for his actions (Zahrā 1995, 36). Fāṭima ʿUmar al-Mukhtār tells of the bravery of women facing execution including a woman who began to trill (*zaghrata*) when the Italians threatened to execute her. When asked why she was celebrating, she said because 'I want to be like ʿUmar al-Mukhtār', who they had hanged (Zahrā 1995, 61). This echoes the interview with Fāṭima al-ʿAqariyya, pointing to the heroism in the face of violence as a central theme of women's narratives.

Individual experience of violence and loss are central to women's narratives and indicate the ways in which Italian actions damaged their social world. The death of male family members had devastating effects on the lives of women because they lacked economic and social independence. Ruqiyya al-Fakhrī lost her husband less than a week after her wedding, and later all her male relatives were taken to the al-'Aqīla concentration camp, leaving her without protection (Zahrā 1995, 109–111). It was common practice among the *mujāhidīn* to marry or take under their protection the wives and daughters of *mujāhidīn* who had died in battle with the Italians. When a man named Muḥammad Būnajī al-Masārī died at the battle of al-ʿAqīr ((Zahrā 1995, 71),[10] his four daughters were put under the protection of ʿUmar al-Mukhtār, al-Ḥasan al-Riḍā and Yūsif Būraḥīl. ʿUmar al-Mukhtār married one of the sisters, Sālmīn, and after she was killed in battle, he married the second sister, Fāṭima (71–72).

While the death of a male family member could leave women vulnerable, the Italian army also targeted the civilian population directly. The Italians used their superior military technology to maximise losses on the Libyan side.[11] A number of *mujāhidīn* recount strafing by the Italians in which low-flying planes used aircraft-mounted machine guns to kill members of the resistance (al-Hāyn 1989, 91). Along with fighters, the Italians targeted the women, children, and livestock of the *mujāhidīn* during these raids, inflicting heavy casualties (94). In addition to the bombardment of the *mujāhidīn* from the air, Italians used Phosgene and mustard gas in 1923–1924, 1927–1928 and 1930 against the Libyan population, despite the fact that Italy had signed the Geneva Gas Protocol in 1925, which banned the use of poison gas and other forms of chemical warfare (Labanca 2004, 311).

While it has been previously noted that the lines between civilian and combatant were purposely blurred under colonialism, colonial powers also obscured the line between licit and illicit action. In Algeria, for example, the French waged a brutal war of 'pacification' against the indigenous population between 1930 and 1947 that included razing villages and the asphyxiation of rebels hiding in caves on the west bank of the Chéliff (Stora 2001, 5). Jean-Louis de Lanessan revealed that the French

> 'consider any village that gives refuge to a group [of rebels] or fails to report its presence to be responsible and guilty. They have the chief and the three or four most important villagers beheaded, then set fire to the village and raze it to the ground'. (Le Cour Grandmaison 2001)

Thus, the French utilised collective punishment as a tool to undermine the resistance to their rule. The Italians adopted a similar policy in relation to the population of Cyrenaica. They routinely burned crops and filled in wells, the major sources of food and water for the rural population (Zahrā 1995, 36). If rebels attacked an Italian position, the nearest camp was held primarily responsible for providing moral and material support to *mujāhidīn*. The Italians destroyed the camps and robbed *mujāhidīn* of their supply lines. Abrīdān al-Sanūsī Brīdān recounted the fact that Italians targeted the relatively unprotected camps the end of battles:

> The Italian attacked the camps of the *mujāhidīn* as they always did after the battles to put pressure on the *mujāhidīn*, and they pressed their attack against the grouped tents of the *mujāhidīn* and there was no one to face them besides women and children and some defenders from among the *mujāhidīn*. Groups of the *mujāhidīn* were called from their various locations to rescue the prisoners and my father was one of them. He saved Ruqiyya al-Mabrūk and killed the soldiers that were taking her prisoner (al-Hāyn 1989, 25).

While Brīdān's camp was fairly lucky during this particular battle, not all camps were as successful in repelling attacks. At the battle of ʿAqīra al-Masīrab, for example, forty women and children were captured from the village of Saʿīd Yūnis Būʿāliyya and the Italians burned all their tents and furnishings. Brīdān's mother was among those captured and then imprisoned in the region of Suluq for five months (21).

While the Italian government had success subduing opposition to their rule in Tripolitania, the resistance used its superior knowledge of the terrain of hilly topography in Cyrenaica to prevent the Italians from winning a decisive victory between 1923 and 1930. In 1930, General Graziani decided to utilise all the tools at his disposal to crush the resistance, arguing that he needed to secure the border between Libya and Egypt and be granted the permission to 'strike at the heart' of the resistance since it currently had a power base in a foreign county, Egypt, which the Italian military could not invade.[12] He devised a plan to cut off the *mujāhidīn's* supply lines from western Egypt by building a 270-kilometre fence stretching along the Libyan-Egyptian border at a cost of L. 13,500,000,[13] or about L. 49,000 per kilometre.[14] The construction of the border fence went along with the confinement of the majority of the nomadic population within concentration camps in Eastern Libya.[15]

Concentration camps

The concept of the modern concentration camp originated in the colonial encounter at the turn of the nineteenth and twentieth centuries.[16] In the Libyan context, Italians frustrated by the hit and run tactics of the resistance, who could disappear within the population after battles and then reunite, devised a policy to physically separate members of resistance from the larger population by placing the tribes under a form of strict surveillance.

This policy of separation started in June 1930, as the Italians determined it was necessary due to the unique conditions in Libya where there was widespread support for the resistance in spite of harsh reprisals. This fact was not lost on the *mujāhidīn*: ʿUthmān Jabrīl Muḥammad Būyamīna stated that 'since ʿUmar al-Mukhtār drew his strength from the people's assistance, Italy decided to intern them in concentration camps' (al-Hāyn 1989, 74).[17] Majīd Yūnis Muṣṭafā al-Jayyāsh also mentioned that 'a number of things slowed the *jihād*'s progress, and one of them was the deportation of the Bedouin villages to concentration camps in al-ʿAqīla and al-Brīga', pointing to the military effectiveness of the Italians' strategy (al-Hāyn 1989, 15).[18]

Hannah Arendt has argued that the establishment of concentration camps was the culmination of a process through which certain sections of the population were placed outside of the protection of the law and deprived of any form of judicial process (Arendt 1951, 447). In Libya, these camps were, in effect, giant open-air jails to house those suspected of aiding the *mujahidin* in the hope of breaking the back of the resistance. The camps were a punitive measure that sought to punish the population for their continued disobedience rather than simply divide people between good (non-resisting) members of the population and bad (resisting) members.

Starting in June 1930, the population of Cyrenaica was confined in 15 concentration camps surrounded by barbed wire between Benghazi and al-ʿAqīla ['al-ʿAgīla' in the Libyan dialect]. The population was subject to strict rationing and control over the grazing of their livestock and allowed to move outside the confines of the camps only with a special permit. In the course of the round-up and internment of the population in 1930–31, roughly 90% of its sheep, goats, and horses and 80% of its camels and horses perished (Gooch 2005, 1020). It is estimated that approximately one-third of the population of Cyrenaica, between 85,000 and 110,000 people, were interned in concentration camps, a large number of whom died by execution, disease, and hunger, in many cases in front of their family members (Ahmida 2009, 139).

Among the many atrocities committed by the Italians, the concentration camps are remembered with the greatest bitterness. Jamīla Saʿīd Sulaymān gives the most detailed account of her life in the al-ʿAqīla concentration camp, located about 300 km west of the city of Benghazi:

> In the camp, it was rare that several hours would pass without a death. I remember my brother ʿAbd al-Raḥmān died of hunger and we shrouded him with a scrap of cloth and we buried him next to us in the sand and the whip of overseer would be raised to any person for the least reason and insults were a common occurrence for the old and young, men and women alike. After I had stayed in the camp for a period of a year and a half, someone came and informed me that my son, Salīm, had fallen from his father's arms after he was taken in the battle of Wādī Shubāriq and had been taken prisoner and taken to the camp as well. When I went to him, he fled from me and began to cry but after a while

when a group of the young orphaned children were brought to me and I was charged with preparing their food and I got closer to my son, little by little, until he trusted that I was really his mother. And the health of the women that were charged with the cooking got a little better meanwhile misery had engulfed the camp and spread in it. We saw people's bodies start to swell and waste away and then die slowly and we lived surrounded by constant terror and death from hunger and thirst, sickness and hanging. I heard with my own ears several times the Italian officers and some of the recruits ordered some of the women, who were asking for a few scraps to allay their infant children's hunger, to throw them in the sea, because the goal was really their death or the death of all of the prisoners. And I did not know if God would spare my life, so now I thank Him greatly (al-Hāyn 1989, 12).

Here, she expresses the feelings of the personal loss of her brother in the camps and a mother's experience of locating her young son. Intertwined with this personal loss is the collective helplessness experienced by the camp's inhabitants and their inability to protect their families from torture, forced labour, degradation, starvation and death. Suffering was indiscriminate and affected all the inhabitants but, at the same time, the collective suffering affected individual lives and shaped individual experiences.

In a similar vein, Adm al-Hāyin Sulaymān al-Qatalā recounted his experience in the same camp:

[Al- ʿAqīla] was a prison of destruction for all, and we would work without anything in exchange. There were entire families that perished from hunger and sickness. I cannot count the number of those that died every day, and I saw women who were suspended upon a board for two days or more and were not allowed to relieve themselves until their clothes became dirty and blackened. Whenever I remember the terror of al- ʿAqīla and al-Briqa, I am filled with sadness because of the painful memories that remain in my soul (al-Hāyn 1989, 47).

These accounts express the feelings of shame about being unable to protect women in the camps from the arbitrary and cruel treatment of the Italians. The Italians used the exposure of women's bodies in public as a form of collective punishment. In a society that places emphasis both on the protection of women and on the concealment of female bodies and physical modesty, this treatment was deeply degrading for the individual women, who were publicly exposed. It was also a social humiliation for male family members in a society that values honour, since men were not able to protect their women-folk.

Conclusion

While the Italians eventually succeeded in crushing the Libyan resistance through the use of brute force, their military victory was a political failure. Rather than establishing the legitimacy of Italian rule, the savagery of the campaign further called into question Italy's image before the international community. As noted previously, the population of Libya had declined markedly due to the overt violence of Italian rule, either perishing in battle, dying from disease and malnutrition, or fleeing across the borders into Tunisia and Egypt. These scars and resentment would continue to be carried by the local population, along with their remembrance of the 'Butcher of Cyrenaica', General Graziani. The crimes of Mussolini's government would not soon be forgotten.

Women such as Jamīla Saʿīd Sulaymān, Mabrūka bint ʿAbd al-Rahmān bin Salīm, and Honiyya Sulaymān Idrīs Abū Baqūsha were a central and important part of the resistance against the Italian invasion, risking their lives and facing great hardships to defend their homes and family and 'answer the call of *jihād*'. While women may not have typically carried arms, they nonetheless displayed great courage and fortitude against almost impossible odds. The Italians purposely targeted the civilian population as part of their policy of 'pacification' and, as a consequence, women routinely faced capture, interrogation, torture and internment in concentration camps. This kind of violence had lasting impact on the lives of women because it destroyed the social world of the Bedouin by disintegrating familial and tribal ties.

Overall, the women whose stories are captured by the narratives participated in the resistance to Italian colonialism through a variety of means. The lack of a clear division between combatants and civilians was a key element of the Italian colonial encounter, as it was an element of many anti-colonial uprisings and wars of independence. Within this context, women joined the resistance for a variety of reasons, but mostly due to a mixture of anti-imperialist sentiment fuelled by religious identity and local allegiances to their families and tribes. Of the women surveyed, only a few took up arms against the Italians. However, the lack of widespread participation by women in direct combat roles in no way diminished their contribution to the resistance. It also did not protect them from violent retribution at the hands of the Italian authorities. Recognising their symbolic value and strategic importance to the resistance, the Italians regularly targeted women and children specifically.

In addition to bringing to light the experiences of women and non-elite groups under Italian colonialism, violence emerges forcefully in this history, although 'violence' seems an insufficient term to fully capture such brutality. The violence of the state against the individual, the strong against the weak, the 'civilized' against the 'backward', points to power dynamics that ensure certain groups of people are dehumanised and brutality is unleashed upon them. This violence is then partially forgotten, sometimes even by the victims, as understandings of traumatic events are constructed through shared, cultural memory. In its most excessive manifestations, women in

Libya experienced the same kind of state violence as men. At the same time, this violence resulted in the destruction of the social framework that offered a degree of (albeit patriarchal) protection in tribal societies. Faced with resistance, the colonial system did not hesitate to release the full ruthlessness of the modern state against the civilian population of Libya, including women.

Much like other forms of power, violence is gendered. While women experienced some similar forms of violence as men, their experiences were not identical. The Italian military habitually targeted women due to their physical vulnerability during skirmishes and battles but also to humiliate their male kin who were unable to protect them. The Italians utilised the Libyan preoccupation with honour as a way to punish the *mujāhidīn* by capturing and kidnapping women and putting their chastity in danger or physically exposing their bodies. In some cases, they subjected women to particularly gendered forms of violence: namely rape and other forms of sexual violence. While their male compatriots fought bravely, their manhood and honour was undermined by their inability to protect their female kin. Once lost, it is difficult for such honour to be regained.

Notes

1. The three Ottoman regions of Tripolitania, Cyrenaica and Fezzan were not known as Libya until 1929. Following scholarly convention, the use of the term prior to 1929 is a matter of convenience.
2. Under Islamic law, once a woman has reached the age of puberty, she cannot be married without her consent. If she wishes to contract her own marriage, some schools of Islamic jurisprudence require the permission of her guardian if she is a virgin for her to enter into the contract. Before a woman has reached puberty, she can be married without her consent but the consummation of the marriage must be delayed until she has reached physical maturity. In all schools of Islamic jurisprudence, the dower is her own private property which she may dispose of as she deems fit (Tucker 2008, 41–50).
3. Jamīla Saʿīd Sulaymān was born in Shahhat in 1900. Her mother's name was Khūaydm al-Kīlānaī al-ʿAūkaliyya. She was from the tribes of Ḥāsa, Shabāriqa, al-Fayshī and Sūayḥil.
4. ʿAtīqa Masʿūd al-Shawayʿar listed these two women along with Ibrīs Abū Mizura as the deaths she remembers from the battle of al-Naḍīd. ʿAtīqa Masʿūd al-Shawayʿar was from the Idrsa and the Zlūṭ tribes. Her date and place of birth were unknown and the interview was conducted in 1983.
5. *Zaghārīd* are trilling sounds made by Arab women as a manifestation of joy or extreme sadness.
6. Hūayna Muḥammad Ibrīdān al-Baraʿṣī was born in 1893. The location is listed as 'mutanaqala' or nomadic.
7. Founded by Muḥammad bin ʿAlī al-Sanūsī, often called the Grand Sanūsī (al-Sanūsī al-Kabīr), the Sanūsiyya established a number of zawāya (lodges) in equatorial Africa during the nineteenth century. The teachings of the movement, which emphasised a pure and austere version of Islam, found supporters

among the nomadic and semi-nomadic tribes of Eastern Libya. For more information on the Sanūsiyya (St. John 2008, 69–71).
8. Archivio dello Stato (ACS); Carte Graziani, Busta 7; Fasc. 10. Sottofasc. 4. Telegramma a Dottor Pomilio, Giornale Azione Coloniale, da Graziani. 27 gennaio 1932.
9. Mabrūka bint ʿAbd al-Raḥmān bin Salīm was from the Būhadī tribe.
10. In addition to the death of her father, her only brother, Ḥamad Būnajwā, died at age 25.
11. Ufficio Storico dello Stato Maggiore dell'Esercito (AUSSME). Rep. L-8 racc. 172/3. Situazione politica in Cirenaica alla fine del 1922, undated.
12. ACS. Carte Graziani, Busta 7, Fasc 10. Sottofasc 4. Da Graziani a S.E. Cantalupo. 10 marzo 1931.
13. ACS. Carte Graziani, Busta 7. Fasc 11. Sottofasc 1. Pro-Memoria per S.E. il V. Governatore e Comandate delle Truppe, riguardante la construzione di un reticolato sul confine orientale. 25 gennaio 1931.
14. ACS. Carte Graziani, Busta 7. Fasc 11 Sottofasc 2. Da Societa' Italiana Costruzioni e Favori Pubblici a S.E. il Generale Rodolfo Graziani. 6 marzo 1931.
15. ACS. Carte Graziani, Busta 7. Fasc 11. Sottofasc 2. Dislocazione dei Gruppi Mobili e delle popolazione alla data 1 febbraio 1931-IX.
16. The term 'concentration camp' first entered the English language in the context of the British camps in South Africa (1900–2). The earliest existence of the phenomenon is usually traced back to the Spanish–Cuban War of 1895–98 but references to *(re)concentrado*s occurred earlier in Cuba, during the Ten Years' War (1868–78) and the Guerra chiquita (1879–80) (Smith and Stucki 2011, 417).
17. ʿUthmān Jabrīl Muḥammad Būyamīna was of the Idrasa, al-Sharīrīq and Imuḥammad tribes.
18. Majīd Yūnis Muṣṭafā al-Jayyāsh was born in Slonta in 1909.

Disclosure statement

No potential conflict of interest was reported by the author.

References

Abu-Lughod, Lila. 1986. *Veiled Sentiments: Honor and Poetry in a Bedouin Society*. Berkeley: University of California Press.
Ahmida, Ali Abdullatif. 2009. *The Making of Modern Libya: State Formation, Colonization, and Resistance*. Albany: State University of New York Press.
al-Barghathī, Yūsif Salim. 1990. *Mawsūʿat Riwāyāt Al-Jihād*. Vol. 22. Ṭarābulus, al-Jamāhīrīyah al-ʿArabīyah al-Lībīyah al-Shaʿbīyah al-Ishtirākīyah: Jāmiʿat al-Fātiḥ, Markaz Dirāsat Jihād al-Lībīyīn Ḍidda al-Ghazw al-Īṭālī.
al-Hāyn, Muṣṭafā Saʿd. 1989. *Mawsūʿat Riwāyāt Al-Jihād*. Vol. 13. Ṭarābulus, al-Jamāhīrīyah al-ʿArabīyah al-Lībīyah al-Shaʿbīyah al-Ishtirākīyah: Jāmiʿat al-Fātiḥ, Markaz Dirāsat Jihād al-Lībīyīn Ḍidda al-Ghazw al-Īṭālī.
Anderson, Lisa. 1991. "The Development of Nationalist Sentiment in Libya, 1908–1922." In *The Origins of Arab Nationalism*, edited by Rashid Khalidi, 225–242. New York, NY: Columbia University Press.
Arendt, Hannah. 1951. *The Origins of Totalitarianism*. New York: Harcourt, Brace and Co.

Atkinson, David. 2003. "Geographical Knowledge and Scientific Survey in the Construction of Italian Libya." *Modern Italy* 8 (1): 9–29.
Baldinetti, Anna. 2010. *The Origins of the Libyan Nation: Colonial Legacy, Exile and the Emergence of a New Nation-State*. London; New York: Routledge.
Behnke, Roy H. 1980. *The Herders of Cyrenaica: Ecology, Economy, and Kinship among the Bedouin of Eastern Libya*. Urbana: University of Illinois Press.
Bernini, Simone. 1999. "*Alle orgini del nazionalismo libico (1908–1918)*." Tesi di Docttorato in Storia dell'Africa, Universita degli Studi di Siena.
Chapelle, Jean. 1958. *Nomades noirs du sahara*. Paris: Plon.
Cresti, Federico. 2011. *Non desiderare la terra d'altri: la colonizzazione italiana in Libia*. Roma: Carocci.
Fanon, Frantz. 2004. *The Wretched of the Earth*. New York: Grove Press.
Gooch, John. 2005. "Re-Conquest and Suppression: Fascist Italy's Pacification of Libya and Ethiopia, 1922–39 1." *Journal of Strategic Studies* 28 (6): 1005–1032.
Guerri, Giordano Bruno. 1998. *Italo Balbo*. Milano: Mondadori.
Hughes, Steven C. 2007. *Politics of the Sword: Dueling, Honor, and Masculinity in Modern Italy*. Columbus: Ohio State University Press.
Labanca, Nicola. 2004. "Colonial Rule, Colonial Repression and War Crimes in the Italian Colonies." *Journal of Modern Italian Studies* 9 (3): 300–313.
Labanca, Nicola. 2012. *La guerra italiana per la Libia: 1911–1931*. Bologna: Il mulino.
Layish, Aharon. 1998. *Legal Documents on Libyan Tribal Society in Process of Sedentarization: A Selection of Decisions from the Sijills of the Sharī'a Courts of Ajdābiya and Kufra*. Wiesbaden: Harrassowitz.
Lazreg, Marnia. 2008. *Torture and the Twilight of Empire: From Algiers to Baghdad*. Princeton: Princeton University Press.
Le Cour Grandmaison, Olivier. 2001. "Liberty, Equality and Colon. Torture in Algeria: Past Acts that Haunt France." *Le Monde Diplomatique* (June): December 16, 2011.
Peters, Emrys L. 1990. *The Bedouin of Cyrenaica: Studies in Personal and Corporate Power*. Cambridge, England;New York: Cambridge University Press.
Portelli, Alessandro. 2003. "What Makes Oral History Different." In *The Oral History Reader*. 2nd ed., edited by Robert Perks and Alistair Thomson, 32–42. London: Routledge.
Richards, Paul, and Bernhard Helander. 2005. *No Peace, No War: An Anthropology of Contemporary Armed Conflicts*. Athens; Oxford: Ohio University Press; J. Currey.
Salerno, Eric. 1979. *Genocidio in Libia: le atrocità nascoste dell'avventura coloniale (1911–1931)*. Milano: SugarCo.
Smith, Iain R., and Andreas Stucki. 2011. "The Colonial Development of Concentration Camps (1868–1902)." *The Journal of Imperial and Commonwealth History* 39 (3): 417–437.
St.John, Ronald Bruce. 2008. *Libya: From Colony to Independence*. Oxford: Oneworld.
Stora, Benjamin. 2001. *Algeria, 1830–2000: A Short History*. Ithaca: Cornell University Press.
Tucker, Judith E. 2008. *Women, Family, and Gender in Islamic Law*. Cambridge, UK; New York: Cambridge University Press.
Vansina, Jan. 1994. *Living with Africa*. Madison: The University of Wisconsin Press.
Vidal-Naquet, Pierre. 1963. *Torture: Cancer of Democracy, France and Algeria, 1954–62*. Baltimore: Penguin Books.
Zahrā, Zaynab Muḥammad. 1995. *Al-Mar'a Al-Lībīyya fī Al-Jihād. Mawsū'at Riwāyāt Al-Jihād*. Vol. 37. Ṭarābulus, al-Jamāhīrīyah al-'Arabīyah al-Lībīyah al-Sha'bīyah al-Ishtirākīyah: Jāmi'at al-Fātiḥ, Markaz Dirāsat Jihād al-Lībīyīn Ḍidda al-Ghazw al-Īṭālī.

Remembering the 'Italian' Jewish homes of Libya: gender and transcultural memory (1967–2013)

Barbara Spadaro

ABSTRACT
The article features memories of home and domestic culture of Jewish men and women displaced from Libya to Italy (the former colonial metropole), Israel and the UK after 1967. Adopting a transcultural perspective, the article exposes how ideas of Jewish, Italian and Arab culture and their gendered and racialized representations are negotiated by the interviewees. Developing an interdisciplinary method for the reading of six interviews, my aim is to offer two interrelated contributions. Firstly, to shed light on sites of transcultural experience marginalised by mainstream narratives of history, namely Jewish homes in Libya and Italy from the eve of the Italian occupation to the present. The article highlights in particular how these memories are conveyed through food and language. Secondly, by examining how memories of homes of the past emerge in the interviews, the article foregrounds the role of emotions, power and agency in contemporary mnemonic processes, stressing the gendering dimension of memory.

Starting an interview with a lady born in Tripoli, I asked a question about the family home. She begun with: '*era una casa normale, come questa*' ('it was a normal house, like this one')[1] and I stopped her to ask what she meant. We were sitting in the cosy living room of her home for the last decades – a Victorian terrace house in Notting Hill, London. My visual knowledge of the Italian architecture of Tripoli and my intimate delight with the English style of the interview setting could just not compute that parallel. The lady said something about a block of terrace houses behind the Tripoli Cathedral Church, and then we changed topic. But after that episode I could not ignore how my interviewees, Jewish men and women displaced from Libya to Europe and Israel in the 1960s, would often recur to that expression when asked about their homes in Tripoli: *una casa normale*, eventually *all'Italiana* (Italian style). Progressing with my fieldwork I realised that *una casa normale* may encompass flats, houses and villas built in Tripoli between the 1920s and the 1960s, according to standards and styles of Italian and European colonial building, which included facilities as kitchens, toilets and bathrooms. Dwelling such spaces, the parents of my interviewees, former inhabitants of the old city of Tripoli, broke with aspects of life in the *hara,* the old Jewish quarter where fellows Jews would keep sharing community baths, ovens, and promiscuity with local and immigrant members of the lower ranks of the colonial society. During colonial and postcolonial decades, the families of my interviewees developed new cultures of the body, of the making and consuming of food, of privacy and family life that would be acknowledged as 'Italian but not quite' – as my interviewees would say, meaning to stress their Jewish background – and that in our conversations they would often dismiss as *normali*. I wanted to learn more about a normative, transnational idea of Italianness stretching across the Mediterranean via domestic cultures and encompassing colonial and postcolonial decades. I asked more questions, and the interviews shed light on sites of the urban life of Tripoli and Rome neglected by narratives of the history of Libya and Italy, yet central for the perceptions of the social and cultural identities of my interviewees. The memories of these homes convey transformation of Jewishness, Italianness and Arabness. Their colonial and postcolonial tensions reverberated into the interview fieldwork through the objects, language and food shared with my interviewees.

This article investigates the making of gender and transnational histories of Libya through memories of Jewish homes. The interviews open into Ottoman mansions, terrace houses and modernist flats of Tripoli, Rome and Israel, featuring memories and acts of transmission of Libyan Jewish heritage. The interviewees are men and women of Jewish background who left Libya between the Second World War and the 1970, moving to Italy (the former colonial metropole), Israel and the UK. Their memories expose practices that shaped the mutual definition of Italian, Arab and Jewish culture at different times in history, from the eve of the Italian occupation to the present. My aim is to tease out negotiations of gendered and racialized representations and foreground the role of emotions, power and agency in the narratives of the past and the processes of identification of the interviewees. More than an ethnographic study of Libyan Jewish homes at different times of their colonial and postcolonial history, this article is an exploration of the transcultural arena in which Italian, Libyan and Jewish memory travel (Erll 2011).

Memory in culture, narratives of history

The article develops an interdisciplinary method to read the memories of Jews from Libya in transcultural perspective. Over the last years, a wealth of scholarship from different fields has been acknowledging the transnational and transcultural spaces in which memory and history move. Historians of gender, empires and migration have been at the forefront of this shift, contending the top-down, homogenising narratives of Global and World History through accounts of embodied, subjective experiences of transculturation. These scholars have shed light on historical subjects marginalised from national, colonial and anticolonial narratives of History (Ballantyne and Burton 2009; Clancy-Smith 2011; Gabaccia 2000) examining intersecting axes of gender, class and ethnic identification and their multiple tensions between the local and the global (Midgley, Twells, and Carlier 2016). Rather than discarded, the national is now being contextualised in wider transcultural frameworks that engage critically with the exclusive nature of nationalist narratives of History. Examining the impact of such narratives in contemporary processes of identification, recent scholarship in Memory Studies has identified the national as but one of the interlocking scales in which memories and cultures are constantly produced (De Cesari and Rigney 2014). Astrid Erll has recently pointed out (Erll 2011) how Memory Studies have long been examining the mnemonic frameworks of national cultures, or the culture and memory of single social formations such as a religious group, a social class or an ethnicity. Developing a transcultural perspective on memory instead means engaging with the movement of people, forms and media of memory across social, linguistic and political borders, and with the multiple possibilities of memorialisation in contemporary culture. The memories of the Jews from Libya offer a unique perspective to explore the transcultural nature of Italian, Libyan and Jewish memory narratives because they intersect them all, exposing their mutual tensions. This article examines such tensions at different times in history and how they reverberate through the mnemonic processes of men and women interviewees.

Jewish memories have historically been developed at the intersection of national and diasporic dimensions, and a new wave of scholarship is now engaging with the sheer diversity of Jewish transnational and multilingual experiences. Historians researching the trajectories of Jews of the Middle East (Bashkin 2014) and North Africa (Benichou Gottreich and Schroeter 2011; Benichou Gottreich 2008) have been acknowledging the intensified activation of Arab Jewish identities in the present, and engaged with their articulation in the past. Recent scholarship on the literature of Sephardic and Mizrahi diasporas (Miccoli 2017) has been giving two important theoretical and methodological contributions to this emerging field of studies. Firstly, by calling for more inclusive and complex frameworks in which re-contextualise the so-called European Jewish paradigm, i.e. the foregrounding of the history of Zionism, of European Jews and of the memory of the Shoah as universal Jewish heritage. Considering Sephardic memories and historical experiences, these scholars have been examining the thriving processes of memorialisation in Sephardic literature, developing fresh research on the tensions between history and memory. Secondly, while focusing on literatures, these scholars also call for a broader understanding of a field 'which goes beyond the primacy often ascribed in Western canons to novels and includes a larger range of writings and authorial experiences that, however, also relate to one another as regards themes and memorial trends' (Miccoli 2017, 4) In other words, while prompting the development of more inclusive concepts of literature, they expose the heterogeneity of media of memory of the Sephardic diasporas, and their intertextuality across multiple processes of memorialisation and heritagisation (Trevisan Semi, Miccoli, and Parfitt 2013). Piera Rossetto's work on the mnemonic processes of the Jews from Libya has fed into this scholarship, examining the re-shaping of Libyan Jewish identities in the public spheres of Italy and Israel (Rossetto 2015, 2017).

There are multiple ways of remembering in culture, and rather than opposing memory and history this article aims to examine their interaction in a wider and transcultural framework. As Erll, Young and Nunning put it, 'there are different modes of remembering identical past events (…) Myth, religious memory, political history, trauma, family remembrance, or generational memory are different modes of referring to the past … History is but yet another mode of cultural memory, and historiography its specific medium'. (Erll, Nünning, and Young 2008). The memories of the Jews from Libya shed light on disregarded patterns connecting Europe, North Africa and the Middle East, challenging neat accounts of nation-building, decolonisation and democracy (Clancy-Smith 2011). History narratives have long strived to build cohesive, neatly defined communities from progressive myths of struggle, survival, national – or Jewish – regeneration. The trajectories of my interviewees trouble neat narratives and definitions of Jewish, Libyan, Italian identities. The memories of my interviews are in constant tensions with them.

It is worth to outline the main tensions that have long underlied the historiography on the Jews of Libya within the wider field of history of Sephardic Jews in North Africa and the Middle East. Early scholarship stemming from Italian (Felice 1978) and Israeli (Roumani 2007) perspective has investigated the history of Libyan Jews from the eve of Italian occupation to the 1970s, representing Europe and the West as driving forces of modernity and civilisation that Jews would embrace and Muslim reject – rejecting many other signs of 'Westerness', modernity and civilisation altogether. More recently, other scholars have been giving more nuanced accounts of the history of the Jews from North Africa and the Middle East, examining the processes of memorialisation of their displacement from multiple perspectives (Goldberg 1990; Baussant 2013), including the Muslims' (Abécassis and Dirèche 2012). Two significant arguments emerge from recent scholarly debates. Firstly: early narratives applied a simplified notion of an alleged 'emancipation' brought to North Africa and the Middle East in colonial times, overlooking histories of multiple modernities, transcultural contacts, and individual Jewish and non-Jewish trajectories traced across the Mediterranean since the age of the European empires. Secondly: scholarship that conflate very different histories of Jewish communities from the Middle East and North Africa into a single tale of 'Jews of Arab Lands' (f.e. Bensoussan 2012), foster the so called 'neolachrymose narratives of the history of the Jews' (Benichou Gottreich 2008), imagined as inescapable destiny of exile and persecution. Written in historiography, these narrative tensions resonate across further circuits and media of the memory of the Jews from Libya.

Focusing on a series of interviews with Italian Jews from Libya, this article intends to shed light on the broader dynamism of their memory, exposing the variety of its media. Reflecting on the intersubjective relation between interviewer and interviewee (Passerini 2007), my analysis exposes the performative quality of mnemonic processes, their gendered and intergenerational patterns. Examining figures that conveyed traumas, fantasies and cultural tensions in the interviews, I have identified three recurrent mnemonic processes: remembering, forgetting and fantasising. I will introduce the context and subjects of my research before entering in the mnemonic processes.

Rooms and hosts: context and subjects of research

The article draws from interviews with six men and women born in Libya between the early 1930s and the mid-1950s, who are now living in Italy, Israel and the UK.[2] Through a semi-structured format, the interviews aimed to explore the memories of Libya and the Jewish background of the interviewees, who contributed to a collection of personal stories of the Jews from Libya promoted by an established Italian Jewish archive.[3] Most of the interviewees staged our meeting in their homes rather than in offices, community centres or other public places, and they would continuously refer to objects and memories at hand. Images of flats, houses and villas of Tripoli and Benghazi floated in the domestic interiors of Milan, Rome, London and Tel Aviv where we would touch objects and family pictures, sharing food that convey their memories. Collapsing distinctions between places and times, images of home and domestic culture underpinned the interview narratives.

The ladies interviewed are born from families of the bourgeois élite of Tripoli and Benghazi between the mid-1930s and the mid-1950s, and they belong to the first generation of women educated to degree level, either in Italy or in Europe. They consider themselves to be Jews, and in many extent, they also consider themselves to be Italian, although they might hold other, or multiple (i.e. European or Israeli) passports. Their families belong to a cultural and economic élite of Jewish and multilingual background that since the nineteenth century would act as agents, business correspondents, and even consuls of European nations. These subjects played a substantial part in the circulation of European languages and cultures in North

African and Mediterranean societies, and in Libya they certainly played a pivotal role in the spreading of Italian.

In precolonial and colonial decades, passports and forms of citizenship were tools of the geopolitical game of the European expansion in the Mediterranean. In 1870 the Crémieux decree was implemented to secure French influence in the area by imposing French naturalisation to the Jews of Algeria: Arab Jewish traders from Tripoli and Tunis then took residence in Algeria for gaining eligibility, and in so doing, they also boosted French demographic power, while Arab Muslims would be progressively relegated to the status of colonial subjects. Similarly, some Jewish traders and businessmen of Tripoli became formally resident of Rome, while keeping their thriving Mediterranean trading business from North Africa. Jewish traders contributed to the formation of an élite of Italian language and connections for the small society of colonial Tripoli, as families of fellow coreligionists would move to Libya from Italy, marrying into local families. In times of European expansion, Jewish emancipation, and elaboration of modern regimes of citizenship which would dramatise the distance between fellow Jews of 'local' and 'European' background (Schreier 2010; Schroeter 2012), the formation of families of 'mixed' (i.e. Italian and indigenous) Jewish background in Tripoli stands out as a remarkable exception (Simon 1992, 5). A new élite keen to identify with the transnational and trans-imperial circles of a modern, cosmopolitan Jewish bourgeoisie that would patronise the coreligionists resisting processes of European acculturation begun to emerge. Some local Jewish families would Italianise their Arab names, found newspapers in Italian and send their children to Italian schools. As a matter of fact, the first Italian school in Libya was opened in 1876 by initiative of a lady of this élite, who invited in Tripoli a teacher co-religionist from Pitigliano, Giannetto Paggi. Yet the tensions between immigrant and indigenous coreligionist which haunted Jewish communities across metropoles and empires reverberated also in Italy and Libya (Spadaro 2015), as manifested in the showcasing of a project of 'Public housing for indigenous Jews' (*Case popolari per Israeliti Indigeni*) by architect Umberto Di Segni (Figure 1).

Umberto Di Segni was born in Tripoli in 1892 in the family of a Jewish teacher from Livorno, and named after the King of Italy Umberto I. As a young man, Umberto was sent to study at the *Accademia di Belle Arti* in Rome and to serve the Italian Army in the First World War, where he lost one arm in the dramatic battle of the Carso (Arbib 2010). Back in Tripoli, Umberto became involved in the designing of many official projects of urban development, including the *Fiera di Tripoli* (Tripoli Exhibition, 1930–32 and 1933) whose housing development was destined to the families of bank accountants and public employees that would make the bedrock of the urban middle-classes. Di Segni's project of public housing for indigenous Jews of Tripoli would not be built, but showcased in a number of exhibitions

Figure 1. Architect Umberto Di Segni, project of public housing for indigenous Jews (1933) as featured in Piccioli (1933).

and publications to illustrate the civilising accomplishments of Italian colonialism in Libya. The housing project was meant to convey an architectural synthesis of modern and local standards of housing. In a volume aimed to showcase the accomplishment of Italian colonial rule, the project is featured as a demonstration of an alleged joint endeavour of Italian and Jewish authorities to provide decent housing at affordable rates for indigenous Jews (Piccioli 1933). Yet despite recurring celebration of the Jewish pioneers of Italiannes in Libya, and the actual linguistic, economic, political and emotional ties of these people to Italy, in their civil rights under Italian colonialism were not to be taken for granted.

In 1940, when the Italian anti-Semitic laws were implemented also in Libya, Jews of Italian citizenship lost their jobs, social prominence, and in some cases their lives. Their feelings of identification with Italian culture and Italy however hold strong. After the Second World War, the families of my interviewees supported, rather than join, the clandestine and mass migration of Jews of lower class and rural background to Palestine and the newly founded state of Israel. They would stress their role as pioneers of Italian modernity in Libya by distinguishing themselves from *gli importati* (the imported people), the Italian settlers arrived in Libya only from the 1930s. Being still confident in the skills, credits and connections to play between independent Libya and

Europe they stayed in Tripoli and Benghazi, raising their children – my interviewees – in a cosmopolitan environment of uncertain political outcomes.

In 1967, when the safety of the Jews in Libya would be no longer guaranteed by King Idris, these families repaired in Italy – rather than in Israel – as refugees or 'repatriated' citizens. Rome was the closest, more familiar and convenient place for waiting and negotiating the outcomes of the political turbulence of decolonisation undergoing in Libya and beyond. In Israel, the immigrant Jews from the Middle East and North Africa would be identified as *mizrahim* and Arab Jews, whilst among the Jewish communities of Rome and Milan they would be named *Tripolini* (Tripolinians). The Italian Jews from Libya would not fit into any Arab nationalist projects, nor category of the social and cultural imaginary in Italy at the time. Since the mid-nineteenth century, the trajectories of these people have been tracking multiple shifts and manifestations of Italian, Jewish and Arab belonging. Such shifts resonate through mainstream narratives of European and Jewish History and through the self-narratives of my interviewees.

Mnemonic processes: remembering, forgetting, fantasizing

Examining the images of home and domestic cultures in the narratives of my interviewees, I have identified three different, and interrelated, mnemonic processes: remembering, forgetting, and fantasising. Remembering and fantasising are examined in the next sections of this article, while forgetting intertwines both processes, showing the dynamism of memory. All three processes capture tensions embedded in the definition of Jewish background in colonial and independent Libya, and how these tensions resonate in the interviewees' narratives. The interviews also illuminate moments of social and cultural transformation around traditional practices of the Jews of Libya, which manifest negotiation of gender and intergenerational relations.

Many of the interviewees from Tripoli lived in apartment blocks raised by their fathers in the areas surrounding the Cathedral Church and *Corso Sicilia*, a busy high street connecting the *Lido* (the beach facilities built in Tripoli in the 1930s) with the commercial and political hub of *Piazza Italia*. Since the eve of the Italian colonisation, their families, like those of the Muslim élites of Tripoli, would rent accommodations to immigrants from Europe, eventually founding themselves labelled as 'greedy Jewish landlords' in the Italian newspapers.[4] As in many sister colonial cities on the North African shores, a new Jewish petty bourgeoisie quitted the old Medina and their quarters of physical and cultural promiscuity, participating in the development of new hubs of urban life.

After the bombing of the Second World War, some of the wealthiest families reiterated this process of social and urban elevation, moving into the villas of *Città Giardino* and *Giorgimpopoli*, two residential areas built during the colonial decades which in the 1950s and 1960s became very popular among British, Americans and international employees of the Libyan government and Oil industry. Some of my interviewees grew up in this neighbourhood.

Remembering: consuming Arab Jewish heritage

In the 1950s and 1960s the 'Italian' villas of *Città Giardino* staged new forms of commodification of the Arab-Jewish heritage of their inhabitants, as it was apparent also in the spatial organisation of these homes. For example, the rooftop apartments of the villa of one of my interviewees' family was destined to the ritual preparation of chickens for the *kapparah*.[5] In the garden, a traditional baking oven reproducing the community oven would be built in a corner to bake the *ftere* (traditional flat bread). Overall, forms of commodification of the Libyan Jewish heritage convey a confident sense of distance from the Arab population, enabling the integration of women of the *hara* external to the families in the performance of tradition. Hence for *Pesah* and other Jewish holidays, women of the old town of Tripoli would be hired to prepare the poultry and bake the *ftere* for the family and guests, since the host ladies, mothers of my interviewees, would be busy with other, less traditional and more sophisticated tasks for the organisation of the party.

Further examples of forms of displaying the Libyan Jewish heritage emerge from the pictures of women and children in Libyan-Jewish outfit (Figure 2).

Figure 2. CDEC Archives (Milan) *Mapping Living Memories* Collection

These pictures, taken at the time of the garden parties in *Città Giardino*, populate the family albums of my interviewees along with older photographs of couples in European and Jewish outfit. They manifest a recurring tendency towards self-orientalizing, or self-exoticizing practices which would not been possible in absence of a confident sense of a Libyan Jewish heritage fundamentally separated from the Arabs. Like the example above, many of these photos would be taken as portraits of perspective brides whom, while raised in suburban domestic environment fully-equipped with goods and facilities imported by their family trades – such as American vehicles, white goods and fizzy drinks – were still expected to perform the role of Jewish mothers and transmit that heritage to their children.

Historians of the Ottoman Empire have read the widespread nineteenth century practice of self-portraying in Jewish costumes as signs of political belonging performed by individuals living in times when 'national belonging was paramount, and in which being a modern citizen of the world was predicate upon being a citizen of a particular state (…) when people around the globe were turning to folkloric nationalism as an anchor in the changing world' (Phillips Cohen 2014, 368). The photos of my interviewees in Jewish costume manifest new practices of heritage reclaiming and self-fashioning, in a context in which the commodification of Arab-Jewish heritage would be wield as a sign of social and cultural distinction. Those photos, along with other objects which populate the narratives of my interviewees – such as the finest Italian *Richard Ginori* china table sets, the silver trays handcrafted in the souk of Tripoli, or the exquisite pieces of trousseau purchased in Italy – compose the material and mnemonic framework of ladies of the Jewish élite of Libya.

The elegant Milanese home of a lady from *Città Giardino*, whom I interviewed with a friend, was one of these settings in which stories of objects would reveal the complexity of these memories. One of the two ladies repeatedly dismissed their lifestyle in Tripoli as *normale*, 'very Occidentalised', albeit 'not quite Italian' and – most importantly – rooted in two millennia of history of the Jews in Libya. The indigenous grandmother of this lady dressed in barracan and was born in the *hara*, the Jewish quarter of the Old Town of Tripoli where the interviewee had never set foot. Indeed, few of the interviewees born in modern flats and villas from the 1940s onwards manifest interest or even curiosity for the homes of their indigenous elders, unless they convey fascinating fantasies, as we will see. This forgetfulness is a resilient tension in their memories, bearing traces of the shifting position of the Jews as members of the white élite in colonial Libya. The forms of commodification of Libyan Jewish heritage described above convey a confident disentanglement from Arab and non-European roots. The interview with the ladies instead provided further examples of the movements of these memories:

Interviewee 1: It was very Italian as a style, and also as a lifestyle ...
Interviewee 2: ... a very Italian lifestyle, unless you wanted to play a joke. Which was what a friend of mine once did, inviting some friends for dinner. She wanted to eat some couscous. Rather than laying the table, she opened it, placing at the centre ...
Interviewer 1: ... a couscous pan! (*couscoussiera*)
Interviewee 2: No, it wasn't a couscous pan – it was a massive bucket, in wrought-iron, full of cous-cous. She put around various bowls with sauces and dipping, saying: 'Here we go, eat with your hands! Put what you want in your couscous, and eat it with your hands!'
Interviewee 1: Well, this was how the Arabs would do! We wouldn't, but the Arabs used to eat this way!
Barbara Spadaro: But in this case, it seems like she was trying something different, wasn't she? What was it? A dinner party?
Interviewee 2: Yes, a kind of party, it was a joke between friends. And in the end she put all that stuff aside, and set the table properly.[6]

In this excerpt, the interviewees recall the experience of 'eating like Arabs' as a form of entertainment in the exotic dinner party staged by a friend. One of the ladies emphasises that the Arabs would normally eat with hands, while they would not; and the episode is archived suggesting that the host lady had to provide cutlery and a full table set for her guests. Both the episode and the emphasis in the narrative mark shifts and ongoing negotiation of the Arab-Jewish heritage of these ladies of the Jewish bourgeoisie. This excerpt illuminate changes in social practices of the villas of *Città Giardino* in the 1960s, as well as tensions underlying definitions of Arab, Italian and Jewish belonging.

The next interview further illustrates how Libyan-Jewish heritage may be negotiated through forms of commodification, particularly language use, and self-narration. The family of this lady negotiated the multilingual and multicultural environment of Tripoli from a very peculiar position, which exposes several threads of transcultural exchange. The interviewees' mother was of Sephardi, Judeo-Hispanic background, the father a businessman from Benghazi. The couple shared Zionist sentiment, and supported the clandestine migration (*aliyah*) of their coreligionists to Israel through the American Joint Committee. This migration emptied of Jews the rural villages and the poor urban neighbourhoods of Libya, provoking also a fundamental shift in the presence of Arab Jewish culture in the homes of the bourgeois families:

Interviewee: There was a deep dichotomy in Tripoli between wealthy people and the poor who lived in the *hara*. I knew about the *hara* from other people's stories, and because that's where our servants would come from. We wanted Jewish servants in order to keep all things *kosher*. Later they all went to Israel, their *aliyah* emptied the *hara*. I remember how I would spend summer volunteering under a lady for the Joint to prepare these miserable people, she helped them because Israel wanted healthy and sturdy people. We volunteered, they all went to Israel, and therefore we had to take Muslim servants.[7]

The memories of the clandestine migration that in 1948 emptied the *hara* of Jewish servants are recurrent in the interviews with women of the bourgeois families that stayed in independent Libya. As previously seen, a few women from the *hara* would still be available to prepare food and Jewish rituals for special occasion, but after 1948 most of families had to hire Muslim Arabs or Italian servants, loosing also this contact with local Jewish tradition and the Judeo-Arabic dialect spoken in the *hara*. As an example, the interviewee explains how in her family speaking Arabic was considered so vulgar that her mother would hire French-speaking servants from Fezzan to police the use of language at home. Similarly, the use of Spanish and Ladin at home would mark the sophisticate maternal background, as the Jewish families of the élite of Tripoli would speak mainly Italian and Judeo-Arabic – or the vanishing traces of it. The interviewee thus claims to have been able to discover her Libyan Jewish heritage only much later, and in Italy. In the 1950s, she had been in fact one of the first young ladies sent to University in Italy from Libya, to study Chemistry, and subsequently she married into an old prestigious Jewish family of Tuscany. In the excerpt below she talks about the unexpected discovery of her Libyan Jewish heritage, which occurred only in 1967, with the arrival in Livorno of some Jews fleeing from Benghazi:

> **Interviewee:** … and there they were, these people from Benghazi, and at that time I was an adult, no longer brainwashed by my mother! So I went seeking for my Libyan origins: I went in these women's houses, learning from them Libyan cooking, how to cook couscous …
> **BS:** And this happened in Livorno?
> **Interviewee:** Sure, in Livorno! Why would I erase a culture just because my mother despises it? It's a culture of mine, and I want to learn it, so I started studying Arabic, talking to this people, their food, their songs … and I discovered a wonderful side, a less Western side maybe, but it's a culture as well, that's it, and giving it up would be silly. I speak Hebrew, and that helped. Then I got a Moroccan housekeeper for a while … so officially I don't speak Arabic, but I do, just few words, and I do understand the language.[8]

In this narrative, the Libyan-Jewish heritage consists of culinary culture and a language awareness developed through Moroccan dialect, rather than those spoken in Libya. This memory of Libyan-Jewish culture is a self-narrative that unfolds two threads of intersubjective tensions: the emotional tensions within the lady's social and family background, and the performance of our encounter. Interviewed by an Italian female scholar, the lady framed the discovery and appreciation of her Libyan-Jewish heritage within the process of emancipation from the snobbery of her mother and the narrow-mindedness of Jewish circles in Italy.

> **BS:** What triggered this process? Perhaps the fact of becoming a mother yourself?

Interviewee: No, simply I was no longer dominated by my mother. And I loved my North African community, it was a tremendous joy to welcome them ... later, even my mother, once in Italy, had to acknowledge that these people are better than those of the Jewish community of Livorno. She would never admit that openly, but we knew that. These people are so generous, so warm! Their home is always open. They are kind, intelligent, good people with great IQ! Think about how they succeed in business in Rome, their triumph over local retailers ... [9]

The lady claims the richness of her cultural background against the social and cultural elitism of her mother and coreligionists in Italy, who would value her European rather than Libyan heritage in first place – reproducing colonial and cultural tensions between the Italian and Libyan Jewish communities. Presenting herself as an open-minded, independent and sophisticated woman was very important in the self-narrative of this interviewee. Throughout our meeting, she would emphasise her ability to value, and commodify, selected aspects of Libyan-Jewish heritage as well as her choice to apply her Chemistry degree in the family kitchen rather than in a laboratory job. As for many other women of her generation and social background, this ability would demonstrate her social and cultural skills of cosmopolitan woman. Yet they also reflect the Eurocentric and bourgeois gaze embedded in her background and historical trajectory. Both would be constantly negotiated by her subjectivity and emotions. At the end of my visit, to complete our conversation, the lady showed me a display hanging in the living room with photographs of couples of extraordinary characters of her family: her jet-setters Sephardi grandparents in a trip to New York, and her grandparents from Benghazi, her beloved *'nonni barracanosi'* – 'grandparents in barracan', as she nicknames them (Figure 3).

Fantasies

A recurrent process in personal and family stories of home is fantasising. Being in constant tension with forms of forgetting and remembering, this process equally reflects the emotional and dynamic nature of memory. Some of the figures emerged through the interview fieldwork bear traces of nostalgia and traumas only apparently forgotten, or indeed transmitted through the imaginative investment of one generation in the memory of another – a process that Marianne Hirsch termed postmemory (Hirsch 2012). Wheter the emotional charge, the fantasies of my interviewees convey in elaborated figures a human desire for memory. Fantasies also expose the multiple geographies and temporalities in the intervievees' mnemonic processes: their clashes and disjunctions indeed challenge the linearity and objectivity of scholarly narratives, calling for ways of reading the transcultural and intersubjective nature of memory.

Figure 3. Domestic display of family portraits: grandparents in NY and 'grandparents in barracan', photos of the author.

The excerpts below feature memories of the same old Ottoman house as remembered by two sisters during separate interviews. The images of this home of French-Ottoman ancestors convey a full strand of family memories and acts of intergenerational transmission, with very different outcomes though.

> **BS:** ... so you don't know which was the house of your grandparents in the *hara* (the Jewish quarter in the old town of Tripoli)
> **Interviewee:** No, I actually know which was the house, I've seen some pictures, and my father explained me that ... I've been there once with my uncle, they still had the soap factory in there. The Arab houses were centred around a main squared court, with the different rooms for the family opening on the four sides. The court was the main hub of family life in the house. My family had the soap factory, whereas in other families women would cook in a corner and the shoemaker would work on the other side ... I remember – and I still have some photos, but you know how people tend to fantasize on this sort of

things ... Perhaps if I could go back with a time machine, I would find just petty, ordinary things, but I remember the beautiful, golden-framed mirrors from Venice, that my grandmother brought along with her. They would hang large and heavy like in a museum. And the flowery Murano glasses, the beautiful carpet, and the two sculpted lions at the entrance. They might well be made of chalk rather than marble but they were rampant, with jaws wide open, and they were massive, same height as my father. The house was named after the sculptures, *la casa dei leoni* (the lions' house). And it had a staircase at the entrance. My mother's house in Benghazi was similar to my father's, but unfortunately when as a child I would go to see my grandmother, she was living in a very ordinary flat (*un appartamento normalissimo*), a second floor flat furnished with a fridge, a stove, a bed and a cupboard.[10]

In contrast with the grandmother's *casa normale* of the 1950s in the modernist 'Italian' quarter of Bengasi, the ancient Arab house of the ancestors in the old city of Tripoli emerges as an enchanted repository of all sorts of objects and memorabilia, a relic of a past that despite all the moving forward in times of intense transformation, was not disavowed by the interviewee's father – with all the ambiguities and every-day negotiations bound up with it. Photos of these old houses are rare, whereas portraits of their inhabitants are common in the family albums of the interviewees. In fact, memory flourishes, via fantasy and imagination, through the beautiful family portraits of 'quite-Europeans' in traditional and modern costumes, nurturing images of enchanted houses as lost treasures in family tales. These are combined with other figures premediating (Erll 2008) the interviewee's memory, often grounded in their personal experience or knowledge. In this case, the interviewee begun with an ethnographic description of Arab houses from which (as she explained early in the interview) she had drawn from family accounts, childhood memories, and recent experience as a tourist in historical sites in Europe and North Africa.

In another interview excerpt, a sister of the interviewee above evokes the same house through similar patterns and images. In this second excerpt the emotional charge of the memory of the old house is very different, as the fading images convey emotions of loss and traumatic detachment from the past. The trauma stretches throughout years in which this family, as many others fleeing independent Libya in the 1960s, were forced to suspend their projects and expectations due to the insecurity and uncertainness of their lives as Jews in Libya and refugees in Italy. Such protracted suspension severely marked the generation of the parents of the people that I have interviewed, particularly their fathers. These men would feel responsible – and they would constantly worry – about the destiny of the properties left behind, the precarious future of their families and their material survival. The last decades of their lives would be often spent in a silence reverberating on their children, through unspoken patterns of inter-generational transmission that recur among traumatised communities. These memories thus bear traces of feelings of loss and impotence, which negotiate vanishing images of marvellous places.

> **Interviewee:** And, basically, the house was abandoned. To be exact: my father always hoped to move back in it, at some point, but they left it when moving to the new quarters of Tripoli. It was a house like those you can still find in Spain. There was a central court that hosted the soap factory, its boiler, and the family would live at the first floor. It was from the 1800, and it was wonderful for those times. My father used to say that the French Consulate held its reception in the salon with Murano glasses … . He used to talk about the day when he went with my uncle at the port to collect these chandeliers. How they were unloaded from the ship … In the house, there was also a piano, and a safe, where my father left some gold, and my grandmother's jewels, her enamelled jewels from Venice, her Venetian corals … everything was left there, there.[11]

In contrast with the image of abandonment, the story of the wonderful chandelier disembarking at the port conveys the memory of busy times and thriving business lead by men of exquisite taste and entrepreneurial spirit. On the other hand, the image of a lost treasure is a recurrent one in the memories of people who were forced to leave behind properties, personal belongings and material heritage, such as family jewellery and other objects that would trace their trajectories across the Mediterranean.

The last example of fantasising intertwines the female lineage of a family and their Jewish heritage, through the written and oral narratives of a gentleman born in the 1950s. Being the last child of a family from Tripoli, and the only member of the family to be born in Rome, his memory of Libyan Jewish culture has drawn from family stories, food and cooking objects since ever. These memories combined with experiences of disjunctures between the tripolinian background and the environment of 1950s Rome, which would be equally familiar for him. Both the interviewee's writing on the family past and his participation to the interview project sprang from a feeling of nostalgia for his late mother and the festive atmosphere of the Jewish holidays of his childhood, 'that I was never able to transport completely in my home' and that he wishes to transmit to his children.[12] His account is firmly centred on the meaning and memories of food for the Jewish holidays, and his narrative structure details the gendered and family roles for the preparation of religious and social rituals, notably the complementary roles of him and his mother. Through a series of vivid and multisensorial images, he describes himself as the dutiful male child of a woman whom, 'with the determination of a tripolinian mother' (*con la determinazione di una madre tripolina*) would send her little child to the *rabbi* with the chickens for the ritual *kapparah*. The poultry with whom he had played on the balcony at home would be slaughtered with much noise and blood in a shiny and immaculate bathroom of the neighbourhood – and the image of himself as a dazed child crossing the street with a bundle warmed by bleeding corpses is still vivid.

Scholarship on the cultural practices and representations of Jews of North Africa and the Middle East has early engaged with the role of food in conveying their memory across media and sensorial experiences (Bahloul 1983; Tartakowsky 2017). Food and its material culture are central to the performance and transmission of the memories of these Jewish communities in displacement: while used in the kitchen, displayed in community museums, or romanticised in a growing number of fictionalised accounts, recipes and cooking objects help to amalgamate scattered pieces and places of memory into narratives that must be transmitted to the next generations (Tartakowsky 2017, 17). My interviewees are no exception, and cooking objects may have a special role in carrying their memories. The interviewee above pictures his mother at the centre of this family heritage:

> I remember her surrounded by kitchen tools that we tripolinians cannot abandon, nor forget, and that my parents brought with them when they left Libya – we had plenty of those braziers and things in the kitchen … They may well hang in a museum today: grinders, some sort of pressure cooker, the metal Palestinian oven used to roast and cook bread, fans … I remember my mother always dedicated to us – the children – to cooking and to the traditions she would learn from her mother.[13]

This mother is remembered as the passionate carrier of a Libyan Jewish heritage conveyed through domestic and culinary culture. Her commitment to this task would triumph over the exotic taste of her cooking, which bear traces of her Middle Eastern, rather than Libyan, background. The latter was inherited from an extraordinary grandmother, who is evoked by the interviewee through a series of mesmerising images. A singer, dancer and independent young woman whom would travelled the Ottoman Empire with fellow Jewish artists and performers until a tempest thrown her on the Tripoli shores. She would subsequently fall in love with the interviewee's grandfather, and stayed in Tripoli with much scorn of the local women, who would disapprove her addiction to smoking, her collections of Oriental and performance clothing and her inclination for European fashion. Despite the initial resistances, the stranger woman, thanks to her lively character and good heart, managed to find a place in the community, eventually becoming a very popular midwife. Today, the interviewee is proud to be approached by eldest members of the Libyan Jewish community who are still mindful to have been delivered in his grandmother's hands.

The images of these two women as evoked in the interviewee's narrative bear traces of Orientalist fantasies, Jewish archetypes and desires of the narrator. 'My mother was really what you would call a Jewish mother – says GG – (…) she adored to be Jewish, and she wanted us to be proud of being Jews, and especially of living Jewishness'.[14] While illuminating trajectories of single women and mothers displaced across the Mediterranean at different times in history, these memories manifest the continuous processes of translation of Libyan Jewish heritage, their gendered patterns, and manifold media, which all convey the incessant desire to transmit this memory – in other words, a desire for future.

Conclusion

This article has examined at two interrelated levels images of home that convey the narratives of my interviewees. At one level, it has shed light on the domestic interiors, transcultural and multilingual practices of the Jewish bourgeoisie of Tripoli and Benghazi from the eve of the Italian occupation of Libya to the 1970s. At the other level, the article has explored the mnemonic processes of my interviewees, questioning how the past is remembered and how this may shape subjectivities in the present and the future. The images of home underpinning the self-narratives of my interviewees expose the emotional and intersubjective nature of memory. As individual narratives performed in a transnational mnemonic arena, these interviews remediate figures of identity and belonging, exposing how memory shapes contemporary processes of identification.

Between the 1860s and the 1970s, the families of my interviewees have traced transnational trajectories across the Mediterranean and the Atlantic, negotiating multiple forms of citizenship and (self)identification. The subjects of this study, and their ancestors, have been identified as Arabs, colonialists, Italians, Semites, Tripolinians, Sephardic, Arab Jews ... Such categories resonate in the narratives of the interviewees, who connect, validate or reshape the figures in their background. The multiple languages embedded in their memories track processes of remembering and forgetting activated by power, emotions and agency. These mnemonic processes call for further investigation of the imperialist patterns of Italian language and culture in North Africa.

After decades of colonial and nationalist narratives of history, the memories and histories of Libya are more active than ever: they are being reclaimed and mobilised by multiple actors and locations. Their multiple languages – Italian, Hebrew, Judeo-Arabic, French, ... - track transnational trajectories and expose the transcultural nature of memory in our time. The dismantling of nationalist paradigms of knowledge now proceeds together with the critique of historical construction of monolingualism, opening new avenues for the study of individual and collective processes of identification. These develop transnational and language-sensitive approaches to the reading of human and cultural mobility.[15] Exploring a series of memories and transnational histories from Libya, this article wishes to take further the study of the movements of History in times of transcultural memories.

Notes

1. Interview to AA (letters indicates pseudonym), London, 8/9/2013, *Mapping Living Memories* collection, CDEC Foundation, Milan, Italy (thereafter MLM – CDEC). All interviews featured in this article have been conducted in Italian, my translations.
2. The interviews are deposited at the CDEC Foundation (Milan, Italy), and they have been carried out in 2012–13 by the author and her co-investigator, Dr Piera Rossetto, for the Research Project *Mapping Living Memories: the Jewish Diaspora from Libya across Europe and the Mediterranean*. This article has been developed within the framework of the AHRC Research Project *Transnationalizing Modern Languages: Mobility, Identity and Translation in Modern Italian Culture* http://www.transnationalmodernlanguages.ac.uk and thanks to a Visiting Fellowship at the Centre for the Study of Cultural Memory at the Institute of Modern Languages Research, IMLR, London. Early drafts have been presented at the 2014 Berkshire Conference of Women Historians in Toronto (Canada) and at the Comparative Literature Seminar of Sydney University (Australia). A heartfelt thanks to Jenny Burns and Julia Clancy-Smith for their generous and sharp comments.
3. For details on the theoretical and methodological aspects of the project see Rossetto and Spadaro (2014).
4. See examples of the anti-Semitic tones of the Tripoli newspaper 'La Nuova Italia' in the years 1913–1916. On the role of Jewish élites in the urban expansion of 'Italian' Tripoli, see François Dumasy (2011). .
5. Old Jewish ritual performed by slaughtering a cock per male and a hen per female member of the family. The meat is given to the poor or eaten by the owners, who donate the value to the poor.
6. Interview with BB and CC, Milan, 11/3/2013, MLM-CDEC. Italian transcription – **Intervistata 1:** Come stile era molto italiano, come modo di vivere anche … **Intervistata 2:** Modo di vivere molto italiano, a meno che non volevi fare uno scherzo; questo l'aveva fatto una mia amica, che ha invitato un po' di amici a cena perché voleva del cuscus. Non ha preparato la tavola, l'ha aperta, e ha messo nel mezzo una … . **Intervistatrice 1:** Couscoussiera! **Intervistata 2:** No, non era una couscoussiera, era una bacinella enorme, in ferro battuto, con il cous cous dentro e poi i vari tegami con i condimenti tutto intorno … dicendo qui si mangia con le mani, ognuno mette quello che vuole dentro il cous cous, si mangia con le mani **Intervistata 1:** Eh, ma in effetti così facevano gli arabi! Noi no, ma gli arabi facevano così! **Intervistatrice 2:** Ma in questo caso era per fare una cosa diversa, cos'era, una festa? **Intervistata 2:** Si, uno scherzo, così tra amici, però poi ha spostato tutto e fatto la tavola come si deve.
7. Interview with DD, Livorno, 14/7/2013. MLM, CDEC. Intervistata: A Tripoli c'era una dicotomia tra la gente che stava bene e i poveri che vivevano nella *hara*. Io conoscevo la *hara* solo per sentito dire perché avevamo le domestiche che venivano da lì perché noi per avere tutto *casher* volevamo le domestiche ebree. Dopo la loro *aliyah*, la *hara* tutta è andata in Israele, e io ricordo che passavo l'estate con una signora che andava per conto della Joint a preparare questa gente di una miseria infinita, lei li aiutava perché Israele li voleva sani (…) Sono andati tutti in Israele e quindi abbiamo dovuto prendere dei domestici musulmani. Ma siccome c'era questa ripugnanza – sbagliatissima! – verso la cultura araba mamma preferiva che parlassimo francese con i domestici. Ma

comunque un po' l'Arabo l'abbiamo imparato, ma mamma non lo sapeva mica, nella nostra famiglia era considerata una cosa volgarissima parlare Arabo. Gli ebrei di Tripoli parlavano tutti Arabo, però in casa nostra si doveva parlare Spagnolo e Ladino.

8. Interview with DD, Livorno, 14/7/2013. MLM, CDEC. Intervistata: Ecco che sono arrivati questi bengasini, e io ormai ero adulta e non subivo più il lavaggio del cervello di mia madre sono andata alla caccia, alla ricerca delle mie origini libiche, e andavo a casa di tutte queste signore, mi sono fatta insegnare la cucina libica, ho imparato a fare il cous cous BS: e tutto questo a Livorno ... Intervistata: certo a Livorno! Perché io devo annullare una mia cultura solo perché mia madre la disprezza? È una mia cultura e la voglio imparare, e quindi ho cominciato a studiare veramente l'arabo, a cercare di parlare con loro, i loro cibi, canzoni, e ho scoperto un lato bellissimo che sarà meno occidentale, ma anche quella è una cultura, ed è stupido rinunciare. Conoscendo l'ebraico, non mi è venuto difficile: non so parlare, ma capisco, so dire una parola o due. Poi ho avuto una domestica marocchina, mi sono allenata ... insomma, ufficialmente io non so l'arabo, ma..!

9. Interview with DD, Livorno, 14/7/2013. MLM, CDEC. BS: cosa le ha fatto scattare tutto questo? Il fatto di avere dei figli? Intervistata: no, il fatto di non essere più sotto l'influenza materna, e l'amore che avevo per la mia comunità nordafricana e la gioia con cui li ho accolti, che poi mia mamma arrivando in Italia si è resa conto quanto erano superiori alla comunità ebraica di Livorno, non l'ha mai detto ufficialmente ma l'abbiamo capito perché questa gente ha una generosità e un'ospitalità, la casa è aperta per tutti, gentilezza, bontà, intelligenza, un grande IQ, perché pensi che quelli che sono andati a Roma hanno fatto le scarpe a tutti i commercianti italiani ...

10. Interview with EE, Rome, 12/11/2012, MLM – CDEC. BS: quindi la casa dei nonni nella hara tu non sai quale fosse? Intervistata: no, so qual è perchè ho visto delle foto e mio padre mi ha spiegato. (...) Allora una volta andammo con mio zio per vedere qualcosa che non funzionava, lì c'era ancora il saponificio. Le case arabe avevano un grande quadrato come atrio, e tutto intorno le stanze per i familiari o del capostipite, mentre nell'atrio, nel grande cortile succedeva tutto, tutta la vita della famiglia; loro avevano la fabbrica del sapone, presso altre famiglie c'erano le donne che cucinavano, oppure chi aveva il calzolaio nell'angolo faceva le scarpe..(...) Io ricordo – e ho ancora delle foto, ma certe cose le mitizzi: forse se potessi tornare indietro con una macchina del passato troverei delle bazzecole, ma io ricordo degli specchi bellissimi con cornici dorate, intarsiate, portati da mia nonna da Venezia, messi come nei musei, grandissimi, pesantissimi; lampadari di Murano con tutti i fiorellini, tappeti molto belli, e all'entrata i due leoni, che forse erano di gesso, non di marmo, ma avevano la bocca spalancata, la zampa alzata ed erano molto grandi, dell'altezza di mio padre, che davano il nome alla casa, la Casa dei Leoni; e poi c'era una scalinata per entrare. Anche quella di mia madre era una casa di questo tipo, ma quando andavo io a trovare mia nonna a Bengasi ormai abitavano in un appartamento normalissimo, un secondo piano con un frigorifero, un gas, un letto e un armadio.

11. Interview with FF, Tel Aviv, 25/2/2013, MLM-CDEC. 'E in pratica, questa casa è stata abbandonata; cioè, papà pensava sempre di tornare lì, l'hanno lasciata venendo nella città nuova, e quella era la casa che rimaneva ancora lì. Era una casa come quelle che ci sono ancora in Spagna, con il cortile che faceva da

saponificio, c'era la caldaia, ecc, e le famiglie abitavano al primo piano, e l'hanno lasciata così com'era. Era del 1800, ed era fantastica per il tempo di allora; papà mi raccontava che il Consolato francese chiedeva il salone per fare i ricevimenti, e mi raccontava che c'erano due lampadari di Murano … mi raccontava di quando era andato con lo zio al porto a prenderli, quando sono stati scaricati; e poi c'era il pianoforte, e una cassaforte dove aveva lasciato i lingotti d'oro, i gioielli della nonna con lo smalto veneziano, i coralli veneziani … tutto là, lasciato lì'

12. ' … atmosfera di cui ho molta nostalgia e che non sono riuscito a trasportare completamente nella mia casa'. Interview with GG, Rome, 03/7/2013, MLM-CDEC.
13. '.. E poi me la ricordo circondata da utensili di cucina che noi tripolini non riusciamo ad abbandonare né a dimenticare e che mio padre e mia madre portarono con sé quando lasciarono la Libia, per cui in cucina eravamo pieni di bracieri, etc. Che oggi potrebbero stare tranquillamente in un museo: macinini, specie di pentole a pressione, il forno palestinese, di metallo con un buco al centro che serviva per fare arrosti o il pane, ventagli … Mia madre la ricordo sempre dedita a noi figli, dedita ai fornelli e alle tradizioni imparate da sua madre. ' Interview with GG, Rome, 03/7/2013, MLM-CDEC.
14. ' Mia madre è stata davvero quella che si dice "una madre ebrea" (…) Lei adorava il fatto di essere ebrea e voleva che anche noi fossimo fieri e orgogliosi di esserlo e di viverlo soprattutto, l'ebraismo ' id.
15. For conceptualisation of mobility, memory and translation of Italian culture across the world, including North Africa and the Mediterranean, see the AHRC Research Project *Transnationalizing Modern Languages: Mobility, Identity and Translation in Modern Italian Culture* (TML) http://www.transnationalmodernlanguages.ac.uk and Burdett, Charles, Loredana Polezzi and Barbara Spadaro *(Forthcoming)*. The present article has been developed under the TML Project umbrella.

Disclosure statement

No potential conflict of interest was reported by the authors.

Funding

This work was supported by the Rothschild Foundation and the Translating Cultures theme of the Arts & Humanities Research Council (AHRC).

References

Abécassis, Frédéric, and Karima Dirèche, eds. 2012. *La bienvenue et l'adieu. Migrants Juifs et Musulmans au Maghreb, XV-XX siècle*. Casablanca: Centre Jacques-Berque. http://books.openedition.org/cjb/207.

Arbib, Jack. 2010. *L'ombra e la luce. Note su Umberto Di Segni, Architetto*. Nola: Il Laboratorio.

Bahloul, Joëlle. 1983. *Le Culte de La Table Dressée: Rites et Traditions de La Table Juive Algérienne*. Paris: A.-M. Métailié : Diffusion Presses universitaires de France.

Ballantyne, Toni, and Antoinette Burton, eds. 2009. *Moving Subjects. Gender, Mobility and Intimacy in an Age of Global Empire*. Urbana: University of Illinois Press.

Bashkin, Orit. 2014. "The Middle Eastern Shift and Provincializing Zionism." *International Journal of Middle East Studies* 46 (3): 577–580. doi:10.1017/S0020743814000609.

Baussant, Michèle. 2013. "Étrangers sans rémission? Être juif d'Égypte." *Ethnologie Française* 43: 671–678.

Benichou Gottreich, Emily. 2008. "Historicizing the Concept of Arab Jews in the Maghrib." *Jewish Quarterly Review* 98 (4): 433–451.

Benichou Gottreich, Emily, and Daniel J. Schroeter, eds. 2011. *Jewish Culture and Society in North Africa*. Bloomington: Indiana University Press.

Bensoussan, Georges. 2012. *Juifs En Pays Arabes. Le Grand Déracinement, 1850-1975*. Paris: Tallandier.

Burdett, Charles, Loredana Polezzi, and Barbara Spadaro, eds. Forthcoming. *Transcultural Italies: Mobility, Memory and Translation*. Liverpool: Liverpool University Press.

Clancy-Smith, Julia. 2011. *Mediterraneans. North Africa and Europe in an Age of Migration, c.1800-1900*. Berkeley: University of California Press.

De Cesari, Chiara, and Ann Rigney, eds. *Transnational Memory: Circulation, Articulation, Scales*. Berlin: De Gruyter.

Dumasy, François. 2011. "Au Milieu et à Part. Prestige et Centralité à Tripoli de Libye Pendant La Colonisation Italienne, 1911-1943." In *La Dimension spatiale des inégalités*, edited by Isabelle Backouche, Fabrice Ripoll, Sylvie Tissot, and Vincent Veschambre, 209–232. Rennes: Presse Universitaire de Rennes.

Erll, Astrid. 2008. "Literature, Film, and the Mediality of Cultural Memory." In *Cultural Memory Studies an International and Interdisciplinary Handbook*, edited by Astrid Erll, Ansgar Nünning, and Sara B. Young, 4–18. Berlin: Walter de Gruyter.

Erll, Astrid. 2011. "Travelling Memory." *Parallax* 17 (4): 4–18. doi:10.1080/13534645.2011.605570.

Erll, Astrid, Ansgar Nünning, and Sara B. Young, eds. 2008. *Cultural Memory Studies an International and Interdisciplinary Handbook*. Berlin: De Gruyter.

Felice, Renzo De. 1978. *Ebrei in Un Paese Arabo. Gli Ebrei Nella Libia Contemporanea Tra Colonialismo, Nazionalismo Arabo E Sionismo (1835–1970)*. Bologna: Il Mulino.

Gabaccia, Donna. 2000. *Italy's Many Diasporas*. London: UCL Press.

Goldberg, Harvey E. 1990. *Jewish Life in Muslim Libya: Rivals and Relatives*. Chicago: The University of Chicago Press.

Hirsch, Marianne. 2012. *The Generation of Postmemory: Writing and Visual Culture After the Holocaust*. New York: Columbia University Press.

Miccoli, Dario, ed. 2017. *Contemporary Sephardic and Mizrahi Literature: A Diaspora*. New York: Routledge.

Midgley, Claire, Alison Twells, and Julie Carlier, eds. 2016. *Women in Transnational History: Connecting the Local and the Global*. London: Routledge.

Passerini, Luisa. 2007. *Memory and Utopia: The Primacy of Intersubjectivity*. London: Equinox.

Phillips Cohen, Julia. 2014. "Oriental by Design. Ottoman Jews, Imperial Style, and the Performance of Heritage." *American Historical Review* 119: 364–398.

Piccioli, Angelo. 1933. *La Nuova Italia D'oltremare. L'opera Del Fascismo Nelle Colonie Italiane. Notizie, Dati, Documenti Raccolti E Coordinati a Testo, Con Riferimenti D'indole Generale*. 2 vols. Verona.

Rossetto, Piera. 2015. "Mémoires de diaspora, diaspora de mémoires : juifs de Libye entre Israël et l'Italie, de 1948 à nos jours." PhD diss., Ca' Foscari University of Venice and EHESS Paris.

Rossetto, Piera. 2017. "Composer les mémoires et recomposer les identités : être 'juif de Libye' à Rome." *Communications* 100 (1): 41. doi:10.3917/commu.100.0041.

Rossetto, Piera, and Barbara Spadaro. 2014. "Across Europe and the Mediterranean Sea. Exploring Jewish Memories From Libya." *Annali di Ca' Foscari* 50 (1). doi:10.14277/2385-3042/3p.

Roumani, Maurice. 2007. *Jews of Libya : Coexistence, Persecution, Resettlement*. Brighton: Sussex Academic.

Schreier, Joshua. 2010. *Arabs of the Jewish Faith. The Civilizing Mission in Colonial Algeria*. New Brunswick: Rutgers University Press.

Schroeter, Daniel J. 2012. "Identity and Nation: Jewish Migrations and Inter-Community Relations in the Colonial Maghreb." In *La Bienvenue et L'adieu. Migrants, Juifs et Musulmans au Maghreb (XVe-XXe Siecles)*, edited by Fréderick Abécassis and Karima Diréche, Vol. 1, 125–139. Casablanca: Centre Jacques Berque. http://books.openedition.org/cjb/222#bodyftn20.

Simon, Rachel. 1992. *Change Within Tradition among Jewish Women in Libya*. Seattle: University of Washington Press.

Spadaro, B. 2015. *Taking the 'Invisible Border' Further. The 'Alliance Israélite Universelle' in Libya: First Insights on a History of Encounters and Representations*, Il genere nella ricerca storica. Edited by Maria Cristina La Rocca and Saveria Chemotti, 251–263. Venice: Il Poligrafo.

Tartakowsky, Ewa. 2017. "The Literary Work of Jewish Maghrebi Authors in Postcolonial France." In *Contemporary Sephardic and Mizrahi Literature: A Diaspora*, edited by Dario Miccoli, 10–13. London: Routledge.

Trevisan Semi, Emanuela, Dario Miccoli, and Tudor Parfitt, eds. 2013. *Memory and Ethnicity: Ethnic Museums in Israel and the Diaspora*. Newcastle: Cambridge Scholars.

Our star: Amazigh music and the production of intimacy in 2011 Libya

Leila Tayeb

ABSTRACT
This article explores the production and circulation of Amazigh music among Libyans between 2011 and 2013. It takes as a focal point the performance archive of Serbian-Libyan Amazigh singer Dania Ben Sasi, whose Amazigh-language music found unprecedented fame in Libya in 2011. Through close readings of her initial musical recording of that year, interviews with Ben Sasi and listeners, analysis of performances onstage and in daily life, and drawing on ethnographic fieldwork undertaken in Libya, Serbia, and Tunisia, I present a brief history of a temporary moment of political possibility. I suggest that the formation of an intimate public around Amazigh music in Libya offered glimpses of an unfinished future in which popular practices of recognition could still be built.

Introduction: to sing an intimate public

12 January 2013 in Tripoli, Libya. It is the eve of the New Year 2963 by the Amazigh (Berber)[1] calendar.[2] An enormous concert marks the occasion, one of the first public events to celebrate an Amazigh holiday in Libya in decades and one of the first concerts in which an Amazigh language has been sung aloud in Tripoli since the overthrow of Muammar Gaddafi in 2011. Khalid Izri, a Moroccan musician of international fame, is joined onstage by Dania Ben Sasi, a Libyan-Serbian singer who has risen to celebrity much more recently. As the crowd erupts in cheers at the sight of her, Ben Sasi approaches a microphone and speaks the Tamazight name of an ancient kingdom that stretched across much of North Africa, performatively marking the space and the audience: 'Numidia!'

The duo performs Ben Sasi's song of the same name, well known among a western Libyan audience. The performance is clunky, awkwardly requiring a number of repetitions of the same guitar phrase before the two performers are in solid cooperation. Ben Sasi has been singing professionally for less than two years and appears hesitant in this collaboration. The audience sings too, swaying in time, some in rows of two or three clutching the top of large Amazigh flags. Between verses, they whistle and applaud. The Moroccan singer Izri takes the second verse alone as she claps and gestures to the audience in support. Izri's – and the audience's – knowledge of Ben Sasi's song offer subtle evidence of the transnational patterns of movement that Ben Sasi's music traced during and after 2011. This movement intersected at various points with the demands of national and transnational struggles for rights and recognition among Imazighen.

The Tripoli audience's enthusiasm is particularly characteristic of a moment of political opening during and just after the 2011 uprising. Interviews broadcast in Libyan news coverage of the New Year's concert centralised the symbolic and political import of the occasion. In a segment made by the Misrata-based post-2011 television channel Tobactus, one young attendee told a TV interviewer:

> For us it was a dream – we never imagined that in our lifetimes we'd see an event like this, where we could express ourselves, we could wear the Amazighi flag, we could sing, we could listen to our own songs.

One of the products of the 2011 revolution has been the increased visibility, and *audibility*, of the Libyan Imazighen in a domestic political sphere and in connection with region-wide media circulation. During the revolution and after, particular recordings of Tamazight-language music circulated widely among residents of western Libya and, as we will see, through networks that stretched into Tunisia and the wider Maghreb region. The people that tuned into these recordings, listened to them, sung with them, and contributed to their circulation, were both Imazighen-identified and not, both speakers of Tamazight and not. Across distance and barriers of nation-state and language, these listeners formed what Lauren Berlant terms an intimate public. This intimate public shared affective ties as it invested in a specific political urgency, thereby both embracing and producing a potentiality that was fleeting and – for that moment – revolutionary.

In *Cruel Optimism*, Berlant (2011, 223) writes, 'Intensely political seasons spawn reveries of a different immediacy.' In these periods, she argues, alternative situations are imagined and 'communication feels intimate, face-to-face' (Berlant 2011, 223). A popular revolution is nothing if not an intensely political season; it is precisely predicated on a momentary shift in which the impossible becomes possible, alternative realities become thinkable, if not clearly fleshed out. In the revolution, which I'm thinking of for the purposes of this analysis as a period of political flux lasting through most of 2011, 2012, and even into 2013, modes of public constitution emerged that disrupted and ultimately displaced the old regime as they offered new possibilities for identification and citizenship.

The public formations that emerged were temporary, to be sure, but filled with political urgency for as long as they lasted. In this way, they were intimate formations. To explicate this idea, it is worth quoting Berlant (2011, 226) at length. She explains,

> Public spheres are always affect worlds, worlds to which people are bound, when they are, by affective projections of a constantly negotiated common interestedness. But an intimate public is more specific. In an intimate public one senses that matters of survival are at stake and that collective mediation through narration and audition might provide some routes out of the impasse and the struggle of the present, or at least some sense that there would be recognition were the participants in the room together. An intimate public promises the sense of being held in its penumbra. You do not need to audition for membership in it. Minimally, you just need to perform audition, to listen and be interested in the scene's visceral impact.

Through the circulation of Tamazight-language music, an intimate public was constituted in which 'members' shared affective attachments. This music directly and indirectly narrated stories of revolution and nation in which North African indigeneity could be both sounded and heard. Its public promised 'recognition,' not in official terms from a state, but more intimately, from others.

Research questions

In order to unpack the production of intimacy via Amazigh music in 2011 Libya, in this article I present performance archival material alongside ethnographic research undertaken between 2011 and 2015 in Libya, Tunisia, and Serbia. Through close readings of musical recordings, performance events onstage and in daily life, and interviews, I ask: how and why did Amazigh music resonate widely – become *sticky* in Sara Ahmed's terms: a site of affective accumulation – among Libyans in 2011? What about this period compelled a burst in the production and circulation of music? How did this moment relate to, reflect, and reinterpret transnational histories of Amazigh activism in the Maghreb? What kinds of political possibility did the circulation of particular music capacitate?

I hope to illustrate that attending to the Libyan Amazigh music of 2011 enables insight into some problematics around identity, indigeneity, intimacy, memory, and recognition in North Africa via a performance studies analytic. As James McDougall (2010, 15) observes, 'ethnicity has tended to be written into Maghribi history as a foundational and causal category,' producing accounts of 'primordial tension' very limited in their analytical value. Recent scholarship, notably the volume in which the above McDougall essay appears, has taken a significantly updated approach to the categories of 'Arab' and 'Berber,' deftly negotiating overlapping questions of language, culture, political community, historiography, and the state in the Moroccan and Algerian contexts. I want to suggest that a performance studies approach to ethnicity in North Africa can contribute to this non-dichotomizing turn by attending to the embodied processes through which identity is reified and contested, both in heightened performance contexts and in daily life.

The fieldwork that I draw on in this essay proceeds from my own diasporic relationship to Libya and this element of (different) shared experience comes to the surface in relation to a number of my interlocutors and Ben Sasi here in particular. I thus make many of my initial contacts through friends and family and I remain implicated in contending visions of future identificatory and citizenship possibilities under a Libyan state. My own performance of audition both drew me to the questions around which this article turns and is one articulation of the claims I make about affective proximity.

I begin below by outlining the context in which Amazigh activism and music in Libya unfolds on national and regional scales. From there I move to a close reading of *itri enagh* [Our star], Ben Sasi's first recorded song, and the circumstances of its production and circulation. The last sections of the article draw from my fieldwork and focus on the politics capacitated by the circulation of Amazigh music among Libyans in 2011 and after.

Amazigh performance in (trans)national context

In this section I begin to contextualise the performance material introduced above and expanded on in the sections that follow. I first situate the moment during 2011 in which Ben Sasi comes to record music for the first time, by offering an extremely brief overview of the uprising in Libya that resulted in Muammar Gaddafi's removal from power and an introduction to the condition of Amazigh politics in Libya prior to this moment. From there I zoom out wider, drawing on the extensive research that exists on Amazigh music and politics in Algeria in order to present the wider context in which Ben Sasi starts her work.

Amazigh politics in 2011 Libya

Libya's 2011 February 17th revolution was so called at the time among participants because it began with a widespread call for public action to be held 17 February 2011.[3] Tunisia's Zine El Abidine Ben Ali had fled to Saudi Arabia in January and the announcement had come just days before that then-president Hosni Mubarak would step down in Egypt. Protest was met with severe state violence in the major city of Benghazi while smaller towns to the east, beginning with Tobruk, rapidly fell out of government control. By the end of February, most of the eastern half of Libya and a few keys cities in the far west were under the control of revolutionary fighters, the majority of whom were civilians up to the start of the uprising. Losses and gains of territory ensued throughout the spring and summer before the National Transitional Council, which was to be Libya's new governing body, declared the war officially over 23 October 2011.

The violent repression of many of the years since Muammar Gaddafi had taken power in a 1969 coup was far-reaching and provided for widespread support of and participation in the 2011 revolution. In a country of large extended families but a total population of only 6 million, most Libyans held memory of state violence, from a relative if not direct experience. Libyans who identified themselves as Imazighen and/or spoke Tamazight formed a particularly thorny portion of the varied opposition to Gaddafi's regime. During the earliest years of Gaddafi's rule, Libyan state policy embraced a Nasser-era pan-Arabism that made most sense if Libya was to be understood as an unambiguously Arab state, as it eventually came to be officially titled in the Jamahiriya's famously long appellation. Even after policy shifted to a focus on the regional power possibilities of Africa, an insistence on homogeneity remained central to state ideology. Cultural policy worked to naturalise the project of the Jamahiriya, in which dissidence appeared to be a logical impossibility because the populace was always already ruling itself. The political philosophy that Gaddafi laid out in his *Green Book* – on which the project of the Jamahiriya was ostensibly based – contended that all legitimate political communities are made up of nations emerging out of natural sameness. That text was unequivocal about the concept of minorities: they are of two types, those who can (and should) be absorbed into the dominant group, and those whose belonging logically sends them elsewhere.[4] The 1973 speech that marked the opening of the articulation of this 'people's revolution' was not accidentally in the Amazigh-dominant city of Zuwara (Porsia 2016, 39).

Thus in attempting to construct a unitary Libyan nationalism in the postcolonial period, Gaddafi declared an absolute Arab Libyan identity that attempted to subsume any Amazigh difference. When pressed on the logic of his assertion of homogeneity, he characterised the indigenous languages of Libya as 'older' forms of Arabic, and indigenous Libyans themselves as 'Arabs who immigrated to the regime before Islam' (Obeidi 2001, 87). Accordingly, only Arabic names could be registered for birth certificates and school enrolment (al-Rumi 2009, 4; Hilsum 2012, 36). In an example of the creative linguistic analysis for which Gaddafi was (in)famous in Arab media circulation, in 2007 he claimed that the word Berber itself shows that these were Arabs who migrated to Libya via land, *barr* meaning land in Arabic (al-Rumi 2009, 3). Regime archaeologists published work in which they claimed that 'Arab Libyan' tribes dated from 4000 B.C. (Chaker and Ferkal 2012, 111). Pointing to the intertwining of Islamic and Arab identifications at play in North Africa, even after 2011 many Arabic-language written histories of Libya take as their starting point the Arab arrival (e.g. al-Ansari 2015). Activists who pushed against these erasures faced persecution in the same forms as other Libyans who did not conform to the enforced performance of regime ideology, with imprisonment, exile, disappearance, and death. Just over a month before the revolution started, Libyan intelligence services arrested four Amazigh activists, two Libyan and two Moroccan academics, neglecting to officially charge them with a crime or allow them to contact relatives or lawyers, but releasing a statement accusing the activists of exporting 'viruses of fragmentation.' One of the Libyans arrested, Mazigh Buzakhar, provided the translation of Ben Sasi's *itri enagh* that appears below.

Music and Tamazgha

The transnationality of the above example of political persecution is reflective of a history of Amazigh cultural and political contestation that spans the Maghreb region, while also maintaining important ties to colonial metropoles such as Paris. While the particularities of this contestation have varied locally, cultural production has been both a shared element of local struggles and a way that such movements have influenced each other. Since even before the Algeria-based 'Berber Spring' movement of the early 1980s,[5] Amazigh cultural-political contestation has had the production and international circulation of music among its central elements. Performance scholar Jane Goodman has demonstrated the way in which what historian Bruce Maddy-Weitzman (2007, 50) has called 'the transnational Berber/Amazigh culture movement' has been 'constituted through and for a world stage' (Goodman 2005, 3). Maddy-Weitzman (2007, 50) has argued that '[m]usicians, poets, and writers have taken a prominent role' in this movement and that some of the more well known of these, 'such as [Algerian] writer Mouloud Mammeri and [assassinated Algerian] singer-poet Lounes Matoub, have become a kind of "memory site" themselves, either as cultural icons, martyrs to the cause, or both.'

The 1973 release of *A Vava Inouva* by then-unknown Kabyle (Algerian Amazigh) singer Idir caused an uproar in Algeria and beyond, engendering among the people of the Kabylia region, according to Jane Goodman (2005, 49), 'simultaneously a sense of deep recognition and a feeling of novelty' while also responding to growing demand among Algerian Imazighen for linguistic rights in the early postcolonial period. It was part of what would become known as 'the new Kabyle song,' a genre that 'emerged in the 1970s in connection with phenomena as diverse as ethnographic film, postcolonial theory, pan-African ideology, and western folk-rock' (Goodman 2005, 3). The song has since remained Idir's most well-known, while Idir himself has become perhaps the most internationally successful Amazigh musician. Libyan Imazighen would have been listening to his music during the same years that Gaddafi's repressive cultural policy was taking clear shape, forming political imaginaries and tactics for activism that drew on the affective resources of their interaction with Kabyle music and politics from afar.

Idir is thus central among the group of cultural-political activists/ musicians who provide the environment through which Amazigh music in the 2011 Libyan revolution should be read. He has also been particularly influential to Dania Ben Sasi, who recounts listening to Idir's music in her childhood as a primary mode through which she began to identify with the transnational Amazigh movement for recognition and rights. Her Zuwari Amazighi father was of the generation who tuned in (performed audition, formed an intimate community) to Kabyle politics from Libya via Idir's musical performances. When it came to passing cultural heritage to his children growing up in Serbia, Idir's archive became a pedagogical tool.

I did not know Idir's music when I first came to discuss music with Ben Sasi and this problem became apparent in our first conversation. In a Skype interview in February 2012, I asked her about learning *tifinagh*, the Tamazight writing system, which, according to Maddy-Weitzman (2007, 62), is a modified version of an ancient script preserved by the Tuareg. She responded:

> Since I was little, [my father] always wanted me to listen to Idir. You know Idir. Idir is the biggest Amazigh singer ever! [...] He is amazing and there are no Amazigh who don't know who Idir is, you know. And since I was little, I was always at home listening to Idir's songs and my father was talking about Amazigh history and that I am Amazigh, I'm not Arab – you know, these things. And I wanted to know more about my nation and about myself, so I was always searching on the internet, and I found Amazigh letters. So I was studying by myself, you know. And it was quite hard because there are a lot of dialects! Dialects from the desert and from Libya and from Algeria and other Amazigh countries. But now they made one *tifinagh* for all Amazigh people.

I quote from Ben Sasi directly because her explanation illustrates both the active project of identifying in diaspora as Amazigh and the centrality of music to this identification. Music, language, and identity ('I'm Amazigh, I'm not Arab') are interwoven in her narrative in a way that points to their interwoven-ness as embodied processes, affective ties, and patterns of trans-generational transmission. Ben Sasi's explanation here also highlights the complex intertwining of local particularity and broad identification that is part of the project of Amazigh activism. In other conversations she tells me that when she listens to Amazigh music from Algeria or Morocco or converses with Imazighen from these places – as happened increasingly after 2011 when she went on to perform in Tangier and with Idir in Paris – she can understand only part of their languages. Yet, still, in her case – because she grew up outside of Libya and does not speak Arabic – she understands them more than Libyan non-Tamazight speakers. She thus falls in an interesting middle position to the contrast that Katherine Hoffman and Susan Miller (2010, 4) describe when they point out,

> What it means to "be" Amazigh/Berber is often different for today's urban activists than it is for rural agriculturalists; activists conceive this category as comprising a transnational ethnolinguistic group, while rural people see it in terms of a linguistic opposition to Arabs.

For Ben Sasi, as perhaps for some of her Kabyle or Shilha counterparts in France for example, Imazighen raised in diaspora who are specifically not taught Arabic as a part of their parents' activism, being Amazigh is a transnational ethnolinguistic identification *and* a linguistic opposition to Arabic-speakers of their 'home' countries.

Itri enagh: *revolutionary, our star*

Ben Sasi was born in 1988 to a Serbian mother and a Libyan father and raised in Belgrade. Her parents met working in a hospital in Zuwara, the predominantly Amazigh city in western Libya where her father grew up. When her mother's visa expired in 1984, the two left Libya for Serbia together, an arduous process because at that time Libyan law prevented Libyans from marrying non-nationals. Ben Sasi grew up bilingual, learning Serbian as well as Tamazight, her father's mother tongue. Ben Sasi's father had long been a cultural activist; he was jailed repeatedly before leaving Libya for speaking and writing songs in Tamazight and for writing in *tifinagh*. Many of his friends left Libya for the same reasons and became part of a widespread diaspora of political exiles. While Ben Sasi visited Libya regularly during her childhood with her mother and siblings, her father always stayed behind, fearing the revenge that the Gaddafi regime was notorious for enacting on those it deemed *al-kilab al-dhala* – 'stray dogs' (Vandewalle 1998, xxvii–xxviii).

The emergence of popular revolt in 2011 thus provoked a nervous excitement in the Ben Sasi family in Belgrade. Hopeful like so many others for the unrest to result in change for the better, Ben Sasi's father became quickly busy following news and communicating with family in Zuwara to the extent possible. Zuwara saw some of the earliest public protests in the west of Libya and demonstrations were met with violent crackdowns. In June, one of Ben Sasi's cousins was killed. When the family in Belgrade heard about the death, Dania's father wrote a song dedicated to him, and to others killed fighting Gaddafi. It was called *itri enagh*, '(The revolutionary is) our star.' During this time, Gaddafi's forces entered Zuwara en masse and the Ben Sasi family in Serbia feared the worst, unable to reach their family in the city. The internet was down, the phone lines were intermittent, and news media was unreliable. They, like other Libyan families abroad, did not know what was happening inside Libya and did what they could to cope. Making music became a part of diasporic engagement with the uprising, a way of trying to feel closer from afar. In the face of the overwhelming experience of witnessing deaths narrated as sacrifice for a shared cause, making and listening to music became a way of trying to also offer something.

When I contacted Ben Sasi in early 2012 to ask if she'd speak with me about her music, she was shocked to learn that someone as far away as New York – where I was then living – had heard of her. Before the events of 2011, she had never sung professionally and her somewhat accidental journey to fame was still quite new. During that June 2011 period after her cousin's death, Ben Sasi learned her father's song at home one day and recorded her voice on her phone. Her father met the recording with surprised enthusiasm and they took the song to a neighbour with a studio and recorded it. Shortly after this, the senior Ben Sasi travelled to Djerba, Tunisia, where many of the families who had fled Zuwara had gathered. He took a few CDs of the song as gifts for their extended family. The song rapidly gained popularity in the camps and from there made its way into Libya.

The studio recording of *itri enagh*, which not only circulated widely in 2011 but has also been frequently used when Ben Sasi has performed live since, begins with sounds of war: shouts – perhaps a protest – followed by the quick rhythm of automatic weapons. A low hum of keyboard strings fades in as the gunshots continue and a man's voice begins to speak: 'I wrote this poem for my sister, who offered her son to the revolution. Today her son is a star in the sky and love for him is engraved in the heart. Dry your tears, my sister!' As the somber tone of the dedication fades out, the start of the percussion marks a shift: *dum ka TEK ka dum dum ka TEK ka dum dum* – it is a song for dancing, heavy with loss yet buoyant with hope. Sparse until this point, the music is suddenly full as Ben Sasi begins to sing. Her voice is strong, pushed to its fullest; a buzz shakes your speakers. Ben Sasi sings her father's words, traversing the age distance between women, offering a brother's comfort from a niece's mouth. Perhaps the pairing of his words and her voice provides what seems a consensus, that in the moment at least there is only one possible way to narrate and proceed. She sings (trans. Mazigh Buzakhar):

Essfeḍ imeṭṭawen-im a weltma	Wipe your tears, oh sister
Memm-im ass-u yesseker tagrawla	Today your son flamed the revolution
Af tmura idamen-is yucca	Sacrificed blood for his nation
Jar itran d ujenna yeḍra	Between the stars and the sky your soul on high
Yura im-is yezzef tinelli (tilelli)	He called for freedom
A yemma slilu afelli	Oh mother, sing your ululations
A tamurt-iw uciɣam ul-iw aɛziz afelli	My homeland, I offered you my beloved heart

This opening narrates loss in the revolution as gendered sacrifice for the nation. Told in Tamazight, and circulated on YouTube with Arabic and

English subtitles, it writes a nation that belongs to Imazighen as Imazighen belong to and within it. In *The Cultural Politics of Emotion*, Sara Ahmed (2004, 133) argues for an understanding of the nation as

> a concrete effect of how some bodies have moved towards and away from other bodies, a movement that works to create boundaries and borders, and the "approximation" of what we can now call "national character" (what the nation *is like*).

I argue that in the moment of the revolution, songs like *itri enagh* provided a narrative and a point of affective attachment through which bodies not previously aligned – or even positioned at odds – could feel close. In a temporary moment of flux, old boundaries are contested and new ones have yet to replace them. In this kind of moment, a narrative like that of *itri enagh* – both familiar in its reference to archetypical themes and unprecedented in the particularity of the current political struggle – resonates, collects affect. It becomes what Ahmed (2004, 11) calls 'a sticky object,' 'saturated with affect, as [a] site of personal and emotional tension.' In its circulation, such an object affects those who encounter it, pulls them closer – to the object and, through their shared attachment, to each other. It produces an intimacy that is all the more deeply felt in an intensely political moment. An intimate public might form through its pull, temporarily listening in urgency together.

Each line of *itri enagh*'s verse follows the same melody until a change comes with the chorus, which has background vocals, much softer and deeper than Dania's voice. The mode of address also shifts from that of an individual to that of a community; it is no longer 'my homeland' and 'your son' but 'our':

Agrawli itri nney	Revolutionary, our star
Yeqqam leyfa win-nney	You restored our dignity
Tafsut n tinelli (tilelli)	The spring of freedom
Tafut n arrac-nney	The light of our youth

Read through the poetry of this refrain, 'our star' is visionary, simultaneously distant and eminent. He has both already acted and heralds that which has not yet come. In these lines – and in the nonlinguistic excesses that can only be alluded to: timbre and other elements of affective force – *itri enagh* shows its utopian feathers. Drawing on Frankfurt School philosopher Ernst Bloch, performance studies scholar José Esteban Muñoz (2009, 3) finds 'anticipatory illumination' in art, 'certain properties that can be detected in representational practices helping us to see the not-yet-conscious.' For Muñoz (2009, 7–8), the 'utopian feeling' through which we can begin to know the not-yet-conscious, is always a forward looking that calls on, even animates, the past. 'Our star' lights an unknown path forward as it retroactively narrates invisibilized bodies into Libya's citizenry, recuperating the Imazighen through the production of a new national project. Such a national project can remain utopian so long as it remains open-ended (in what Bloch calls openness that is kept open).

Between bodies: circulation and intimacy

I first encountered *itri enagh*, along with a few other songs that Ben Sasi had recorded by then, in Tripoli in October 2011. One of my cousins played the song for me on his car stereo as we sped around the city, neither of us able to understand the words. At least five different people introduced Ben Sasi's music to me during that visit, and while some of them had parents (particularly fathers) from the Nafusa mountain region who spoke Tamazight, none of the young people themselves did, having learned only Arabic at home, as was common in mixed families and especially common in Tripoli. My girl cousins especially had embraced Ben Sasi's music in 2011 as part of an emerging set of identifications; faced with long hours and days stuck at home during the months of unrest, these young women put themselves to work learning *tifinagh* and lists of vocabulary. During my visits I would often leave with my name or 'Libya' composed in colourful *tifinagh* on a piece of notebook paper. We spoke about this, a new way of understanding each other as I struggled to learn my father's language and they struggled to learn theirs.

Having arrived in Tripoli after three weeks in the eastern city of Benghazi interviewing musicians, I found a different climate of music production there, one that reflected the starkly different experiences of the revolution that the two cities had undergone. While in Benghazi, which had been free of Gaddafi control almost uninterrupted since February, musicians were collaborating to produce and circulate lots of music, some very optimistic about the revolution, in Tripoli, where Gaddafi's regime held strong until late August, music in support of the revolution had only just begun to circulate freely. For those months before Tripoli fell, music for the revolution, like other expressions of dissent, was passed surreptitiously as people moved across the lines of government and rebel-controlled territories.[6] Which places were controlled by who changed with fighting and movement out of Libya into Tunisia was not one way; often men would flee into Tunisia only to return and join a battalion fighting against Gaddafi's forces. Two of my cousins in Tripoli were examples of this; accused of traitorous activity because of the satellite dish atop their house, they were arrested by Gaddafi police, interrogated and beaten before they were released and fled across the border seeking safety and medical attention. Djerba, the Tunisian island resort town-turned refugee camp had become a hub for many in similar circumstances and within a few weeks they had crossed back into Libya armed.

It was in this context that Ben Sasi's recording of *itri enagh* travelled from Djerba into Libya and it is to this context that the song speaks. The movements of those tied to Libya were multiple – refugees fled; children of the diaspora went 'back,' many for the first time;[7] young non-Tamazight speakers began to learn their parents' language. These movements were both fundamentally improvisational and deeply affective. People with great stakes in the revolution moved the song as they were moved by it. In this way, Ben Sasi's music shaped the space between particular bodies, creating an intimate community, affective proximity, between places as far removed as Zuwara, Belgrade, Djerba, and New York. Another way of describing this would be in the terms feminist geographer Doreen Massey (1994, 7) used when she argued, 'localities can in a sense be present in one another, both inside and outside at the same time.' For Massey, to understand place it is necessary to stress 'the construction of specificity through interrelations rather than through the imposition of boundaries and the counterposition of one identity *against* another.' The overlapping and broadly departing lines that tracing the circulation of Ben Sasi's music reveals map these inter-relations in a way that confounds binarized discussions of 'local' versus 'global' media movement.

Initially, Ben Sasi's music circulated non-commercially. Like much of the rest of the popular archive constructed during the 2011 revolution, it travelled hand to hand, sometimes over email, and when power and internet were cut, from hard disk to hard disk via USB. Once in MP3 form, it moved rapidly and diffusely, circulating, as Jonathan Sterne (2012, 195) illustrates, 'in ways that it otherwise couldn't.' Like other of Ben Sasi's songs, as well as footage of live performance, *itri enagh* reached some via YouTube, where images of Libyan and Amazighi flags flashed in between photos of weaponry, men marching, civilians protesting, and multilingual text explicated the specificity of its relationship to the revolution in Libya. With over 99,000 views at the time of this writing, the YouTube video extended the circulation of Ben Sasi's music in additional ways, certainly to audiences who wouldn't otherwise have known to look for it. Michael Strangelove (2010, 4) has argued that YouTube constitutes both 'an intense emotional experience' and 'a social space.' I would argue that the move to and through YouTube should be analysed as a distinct phase in the circulation of Amazigh music related to the 2011 Libyan revolution, one which drew out certain (especially transnational) relations while it may have overshadowed others.

The processes through which Ben Sasi's music circulated were characteristic of the art being produced during this period in and around the Libyan revolution, processes which in many instances resulted in a work becoming a kind of community property – an affective commons onto which interpretations of the revolution were projected and reflected. An image, for example, of a woman's face painted in the colours of the new/old Libyan flag, and bearing symbols of the Tunisian and Egyptian flags, circulated and was redrawn onto wall after wall such that ascertaining its 'original' would be

Figure 1. Lady of the 2011 uprisings.

fruitless, if possible (Figure 1).[8] While Ben Sasi's name did become known, I argue that her work moved in a similar fashion, one which created an affect of communal ownership. Perhaps especially for non-Tamazight speaking listeners, a wide range of desires and visions could be projected onto these songs, allowing them to symbolise an imagined relation particular to the listener, and later an atmospheric memory of a particular moment. This sense of communal ownership not only shaped how listeners interacted with the songs, but also how they interacted with each other.

Conclusion: intimate recognition

Political theorist and Yellowknives Dene First Nation member Glen Coulthard has cogently examined the limits of the contemporary paradigm of recognition for indigenous politics in the Canadian context. There he describes (2007, 438) 'recognition-based models of liberal pluralism that seek to reconcile Indigenous claims to nationhood with Crown sovereignty via the accommodation of Indigenous identities in some form of renewed relationship of the Canadian state.' These models, he argues (2007, 439), are unable to produce the reciprocity they promise, and instead 'reproduce the very configurations of colonial power that Indigenous people's demands for recognition have historically sought to transcend' through the production of psycho-affective attachments to 'master-sanctioned forms of recognition.' In other words, these politics of recognition generate identification with the very same colonial state against which indigenous claims to sovereignty are in contention.

In the introduction to this essay, I cited Lauren Berlant (2011, 226, emphasis added) when she explains that intimate publics offer the sense that 'collective mediation through narration and audition might provide some routes out of the impasse and the struggle of the present, *or at least some sense that there would be recognition were the participants in the room together.*' I bring Coulthard in here in order to try to more clearly flesh out what an intimate politics of recognition might look like, or feel like, and what it might do. A social scientist would be justified in reading this essay and asking, where is the discussion of Amazigh participation in or protest of the constitution-drafting process? What kind of material change has the change in governance provided for Libyan Imazighen? What does music have to do with material change?

I want to suggest that the intimate public created through Amazigh music during the Libyan revolution helped to suggest foundational structures on which longer-term political projects might (still) be built. I am talking here about popular structures, the kind of recognition Berlant describes above, practices of narration and listening that are temporary but the repetition of which can build paths that may lead somewhere new. In the (too) short term, Ben Sasi's success was part of what enabled events in Libya like the one described at the start of this essay, a concert which featured Moroccan Amazighi Khaled Izri and Algerian Amazighi Takfarinas alongside Ben Sasi, Libyan-Tunisian Arabophone singer Asma Salim, and Libyan Tuareg musicians. This event was part of a period in which staged performances in Libya's largest cities became widespread and varied, a period that represented an extraordinary change from the state-sponsored spectacles of the prior decades. The enthusiastic writing in an article from the briefly prolific Tripoli-based newspaper Libya Herald perhaps inadvertently illustrated this event's affective-political significance, saying of Ben Sasi's *itri enagh*, 'It has become famous and is sung by non-Amazigh speakers too which makes it fabulous.'

Coulthard suggests that the beginning of an alternative to the liberal politics of recognition might start with practices of self-recognition. I think that what was so special about the moment in which Ben Sasi's music circulated – a moment which the circulation of that music also helped to produce – was that, *briefly*, Amazigh- and Arab-identified Libyans found themselves working together on a collective project of revolution that enabled an inclusive self-recognition. Put otherwise, the liberatory act of overthrowing a dictator made for a temporary 'we' against a larger other that allowed some defences to drop and some additional voices to become audible. This was a break, one from which the pendulum backswing has been forceful. In the more recent period after the revolution, a strange misuse of the term 'racism' surrounds Amazigh activism in Libya at a popular level. Or perhaps this misuse predated 2011 and has come back with a vengeance. Claims to Amazigh difference are met with accusations of racism by Arab-identified Libyans, who seem when making these accusations to have internalised Gaddafi's politics of homogeneity. I've encountered an array of interlocutors who either make or report these kinds of accusations. The logic appears to be, if you are saying you are not like me, if you are saying you are different from me, you are racist. I find this confusion about what constitutes racism disturbing, and one of a number of reasons to investigate the period of political opening described in this essay in order to seek insights toward a more open future. What kind of intimate community could be formed in the current circumstances of on-going civil war? What kind of popular practices of recognition might reintroduce 'fabulousness' to Libyan politics?

Those who took up Ben Sasi's songs, gave them love, performed a revolutionary Libyan-ness that created potentiality, a brief sensation – a sound perhaps – of how the world might be otherwise. Ben Sasi's music engaged participants in a way that temporarily disrupted colonial identity categories of 'Arab' and 'Berber' through the collective project of revolution. Not only were those members of two generations who had variously retained or lost Tamazight made more visible/ audible through the circulation of this music and the conversations it encouraged, but further, the temporary sense of unity constructed through the struggle to overthrow the dictator broke open avenues for listening that were otherwise closed off. New possibilities for intimacy were created at the same time that already existing intimacies were shone more light.

Notes

1. I use the term *Amazigh* in various forms to describe people (singular *Amazigh* or the Arabized *Amazighi*, plural *Imazighen*), language (*Tamazight*), and culture (*Amazigh*) in favour of *Berber*, following the strong preferences of my interlocutors. These terms were broadened from local dialects beginning in the 1930s and 1940s and used to identify a pan North African indigenous group (*Imazighen*, 'free men') (Goodman 10–11), a political project that continues to hold import, as this paper elaborates. The term refers collectively to a number of linguistic communities across Morocco, the Canary Islands, Mauritania, Algeria, Mali, Tunisia, Niger, Libya, and Egypt. It is the most commonly used term among members of these communities in Libya, and is generally highly preferred over Berber, which retains pejorative articulations in Arabic and Latin yet persists in English-language scholarship. In using only descriptors stemming from *Amazigh*, I follow what I understand to be a tenet in my home field of performance studies to undertake politically-engaged scholarship that takes as fundamental the worldviews of my interlocutors. For a useful summary of the various languages encompassed by the term Tamazight, and their estimated number of speakers, see Maddy-Weitzman (2011, 2–3).
2. Bruce Maddy-Weitzman (2007, 53) locates the starting point of the Amazighi calendar at the 945 BC founding of a '"Libyan" pharoanic dynasty' by Sheshounk I and points to the Paris-based Académie Berbère as an initial proponent of this calendar.
3. See Hilsum (2012, 12). Protests actually began two days earlier, on February 15th.
4. I suspect that the two problematic categories Gaddafi may have had in mind when formulating this logic were 'Berber' on the first hand and 'Jew' on the second.

5. For an excellent description of the 'Berber Spring' in all its complexity, see Goodman (2005, 29–48).
6. For testimony of individuals who moved between government and rebel-held territory, as well as outside of Libya and back, see Pasmantier (2011).
7. Some of the most prominent of these 'returners' have been musicians. Two US-raised hip hop artists, for example, travelled to Libya for the first time during or after the 2011 revolution. Both children of well-known dissidents, Khaled M. and Malek L. have produced work addressing their 'homecomings' to Libya. The former made a film of his first visit, while the second travelled during the war, settled in Benghazi, and began collaborating with local musicians there.
8. This image uses gendered nationalist imagery in a way that simultaneously pushes at the nation-state's boundaries in its linking of three revolutions, reflecting a particularly 2011 iteration of pan-Arabism. As Sara Ahmed reminds us, 'this conflation of the face of the nation with the face of a woman has a long history and points to the gendering of what the nation takes to be as itself (the masculine subject) through what is has (the feminine object). The figure of the woman is associated with beauty and appearance, and through her, the nation appears for and before others' (Ahmed 2004, 136).

Acknowledgements

Tanmirt! to Dania for our many warm conversations, and to Mazigh for translating, engaging my many questions, and being always so generous with sources. To the conference participants who have engaged with earlier versions of this writing. To Barbara and Katrina for careful reading and precise editing. To the many who continue to work toward a future replete with difference.

Disclosure statement

No potential conflict of interest was reported by the authors.

Funding

This work was supported by the Buffett Institute for Global Studies at Northwestern University.

References

Ahmed, Sara. 2004. *The Cultural Politics of Emotion*. New York: Routledge.
al-Ansari, Ahmed Bek al-Na'ib. 2015. *al-manhal al-'athab fi tarikh tarablus al-gharb*. Tripoli: Dar Fergiani.
al-Rumi, Aisha (pseudonym). 2009. *Libyan Berbers Struggle to Assert Their Identity Online. Arab Media Society*. Oxford: The Middle East Center at St. Antony's College.
Berlant, Lauren. 2011. *Cruel Optimism*. Durham: Duke University Press.
Chaker, Salem, and Ferkal Masin. 2012. "Berbères de Libye: un Paramètre Méconnu, une Irruption Politique Inattendue." *Politique Africaine* 125: 105–126.

Coulthard, Glen S. 2007. "Subjects of Empire: Indigenous Peoples and the 'Politics of Recognition' in Canada." *Contemporary Political Theory* 6: 437–460. doi:10.1057/palgrave.cpt.9300307.

Goodman, Jane E. 2005. *Berber Culture on the World Stage: From Village to Video*. Bloomington: Indiana University Press.

Hilsum, Lindsey. 2012. *Sandstorm: Libya in the Time of Revolution*. New York: The Penguin Press.

Hoffman, Katherine E., and Susan Gilson Miller, eds. 2010. *Berbers and Others: Beyond Tribe and Nation in the Maghrib*. Bloomington: Indiana University Press.

Maddy-Weitzman, Bruce. 2007. "Berber/Amazigh Memory Work." In *The Maghrib in the New Century: Identity, Religion, and Politics*, edited by Bruce Maddy-Weitzman, and Daniel Zisenwine, 50–71. Gainesville, FL: University Press of Florida.

Maddy-Weitzman, Bruce. 2011. *Berber Identity Movement and the Challenge to North African States*. Austin, TX: University of Texas Press.

Massey, Doreen. 1994. *Space, Place, and Gender*. Minneapolis: University of Minnesota Press.

McDougall, James. 2010. "Histories of Heresy and Salvation: Arabs, Berbers, Community, and the State." In *Berbers and Others: Beyond Tribe and Nation in the Maghrib*, edited by Katherine E. Hoffman, and Susan Gilson Miller, 15–38. Bloomington: Indiana University Press.

Muñoz, José Esteban. 2009. *Cruising Utopia: The Then and There of Queer Futurity*. New York: New York University Press.

Obeidi, Amal. 2001. *Political Culture in Libya*. Richmond: Curzon Press.

Pasmantier, Deborah. 2011. "Many Roads to Defection in Regime-Held Western Libya." *The Times of Malta/ AFP*, July 25.

Porsia, Nancy. 2016. "The Imazighen in Libya: From Key Ally for the Italian Colonisers to Inconvenient Interlocutor for the Italian Government." In *Decolonising the Mediterranean: European Colonial Heritages in North Africa and the Middle East*, edited by Gabriele Proglio, 35–44. Newcastle upon Tyne: Cambridge Scholars Publishing.

Sterne, Jonathan. 2012. *MP3: The Meaning of a Format*. Durham: Duke University Press.

Strangelove, Michael. 2010. *Watching YouTube: Extraordinary Videos by Ordinary People*. Toronto: University of Toronto Press.

Index

Note: Page numbers in *italics* indicate illustrations, and the suffix 'n' indicates a note.

2011 revolution 91, 93–5, 96, 97, 100–1, *102*, 103

'Abd al-Rahmān bin Salīm, Mabrūka bint 56, 63
Abū Baqūsha, Honiyya Sulaymān Idrīs 57, 63
Abu-Lughod, Lila 50
Adadi, Abraham 22
Ahmed, Sara 92, 99, 105n8
Akohen, Mordechai 30
al-'Aqīla concentration camp 58, 59, 61–2
al-Halīqīma, battle of 54
al-Ḥaqīfāt, battle of 56
al-Qarun, battle of 53
Algeria/Algerians 25, 34, 59, 72, 92–3, 95, 96, 103, 104n1
Amazigh music 90–106; *see also* Imazighen
al-'Amīsha, Mabrūka 54
Anatolia 25, 26, 35
anthropological analysis 24, 26–30, 33, 40
al-'Aqariyya, Fāṭima 59
'Aqīra al-Masīrab, battle of 60
Arab as identity category 84, 92–3, 94–5, 96, 103, 104
Arab Jewish identities 69, 71, 72, 74, 75–9, 84
Arab state, Libya as 94–5
Arabic language 78, 94–5, 97, 98–9, 100, 104n1
Arbib, Esther ('Queen Esther') 15, 35
Arbib, Mezeltobe 15
Arendt, Hannah 61

Balkans 26, 35
al-Baraʿṣī, Hūayna Muḥammad Ibrīdān 55
Bashkin, Orit 1
bathing 7–8, 30–1, 68
Bedouin 50, 52, 53, 61, 63
Behnke, Roy G. 50, 51

Ben Ali, Zine El Abidine 93
Ben Sasi, Dania 90–1, 93, 95, 96–102, 103, 104
Benghazi 19, 55, 61, 71, 73–4, 77, 78, 79, 81, 84, 93, 100, 105n7
'Berber Spring' 95
Berbers 10, 15, 90, 92–3, 94, 95, 97, 104; *see also* Amazigh music; Imazighen
Berlant, Lauren 91, 92, 102–3
Bini, Elisabetta 2, 29
Blili Temime, Leïla 26
Bloch, Ernst 99
Bock, Gisela 25
body, the female 6–8, 9, 12, 29, 57, 58, 62, 64, 68
Brīdān, Abrīdān al-Sanūsī 60
Bu Meliana 11
Būqafīfa, Mabrūka Yūnis 54
Bursa 26
Būyamīna, 'Uthmān Jabrīl Muḥammad 60–2
Buzakhar, Mazigh 95

Cairo 29, 35
Canada 102
chemical weapons 50, 59
chronicles 2, 26–30, 31
circumcision 22, 36–7
Città Giardino 74–5, 76, 77
city councils 27, 28, 31, 32, 36, 39
Clancy-Smith, Julia 2, 29, 35
clothing: Jewish, colonial and postcolonial periods 75–6, *75*; Jewish, late Ottoman period 6–7, *8*; pastoral women in Cyrenaica 50–1
colonial period 1, 2, 25, 35, 47–66, 67–8, 72–3, 74–5, 76
concentration (internment) camps 47, 48, 50, 58, 60–2, 63
concubines 35, 58; *see also* prostitution
Constantine (Algeria) 34, 37

cooking 8–9, 11, 51, 53, 62, 78, 80, 83
Coulthard, Glenn 102, 103
court records 26, 27, 38
Crémieux decree 72
Cyrenaica 25, 47–66

Damascus 28
dayanim (judges in the Jewish court of law) 11–12, 18
Deriana 53
Derna 55
Di Segni, Umberto 72–3, *73*
Disir village 7
divorce 18, 28, 34, 37, 38
dowries 6, 33–4, 37, 51

Egypt 48, 58, 60, 63, 93, 104n1
El-Ageli, Najlaa 3
Erll, Astrid 69, 70
Esther, Queen (Esther Arbib) 15, 35
European influences 13, 31, 67–8, 70, 71–2, 79, 83
European Jews 18, 19, 20, 69, 71–2, 73–4
Europeans in Libya 36, 38–9

al-Fakhrī, Ruqiyya 58, 59
Fanon, Franz 56
fantasies 71, 74, 79–84
al-Faqih Hasan, Hasan 27, 33, 39
Fascists 55
fasting 21
Fay, Mary Ann 35
Federzoni, Luigi 55
feminist approaches 2, 3, 24–5, 101
Féraud, Charles 35
Fezzan 25, 64n1, 78
flour grinding 9, 22, 51
food 9, 68, 78; as conveyor of memory 67, 71, 82–3; *see also* cooking
forgetting 71, 74, 76, 79, 84
France/French 25, 35, 47, 59, 72, 78, 80, 82, 84, 85n7, 95, 97

Gaddafi (Qaddafi), Muammar 49–50, 54, 93, 94, 96, 97, 100, 103
gender 1–4; gendered nationalist imagery 101–2, *102*; gendered space among late Ottoman Jews 5–23; in Ottoman Tripoli 24–46; and separation 6, 8, 12–13, 16, 18, 19, 52; and transcultural memory 67–89; and violence under Italian colonial rule 47–66
Gerber, Haim 26

Gharian 8
Ghoma (Berber rebel chief) 15
Goldberg, Harvey 30
Goodman, Jane 95
Graziani, Rodolfo 48, 55–6, 60, 63
grinding flour 9, 22, 51
Guéchi, Fatima 34, 37
guilds 28, 30

Hacohen, Mordecai 8, 10, 13–14, 16
hijabs 50
Hirsch, Marianne 79
Hoffman, Katherine 97
Homs 55
honour 48, 50, 64; men's 48, 50, 56, 58, 62, 64; women's 28, 29, 36, 38, 39, 40, 48, 54–5

Idir 95–6
Idris, King 74
Imazighen 91, 94, 95, 96, 97, 98–9; *see also* Amazigh music; Berbers
Imber, Colin 33–4
inheritance 33, 34, 37
internment (concentration) camps 47, 48, 50, 58, 60–2, 63
intimacy 27, 28, 29, 40, 90–106
Irzi, Khalid 90–1
Israel 67, 68, 70, 71, 73, 74, 77
Istanbul 25, 26, 27, 28, 35
Italian period 1, 12, 13, 14, 25, 47–66, 67–89, *73*
Italy, Jewish Libyans in 2, 67, 68, 70, 71, 72, 74, 78–9, 82
itri enagh '(The revolutionary is) our star' (song) 98–101
Izri, Khaled 103

Jamahiriya 94
al-Jayyāsh, Majīd Yūnis Muṣṭafā 61
Jebel Nefusa 7, 8, 9, 10, 11, 12, 13–14, 16
Jebel Yefren 10, 16
Jewish Libyans 2, 104n4; 'Italian' homes in Libya, 1967–2013 67–89, *73*, *75*, *80*; in Italy 2, 67, 68, 70, 71, 72, 74, 78–9, 82; in late Ottoman period 5–23; in Ottoman Tripoli 30, 31, 35, 36
Johnson, Cheryl 25
Journal of Women's History 25
Juhayder, ʿAmmar 27

Khalfon, Shelomoh and Aziza 6
al-Khashabī, Maryam Saʿd 52, 54

Khoms 11, 19
al-Kuzza, Khuzna ʿAbd al-Salām 54

Lafi, Nora 24–46
Lanessan, Jean-Louis de 59
Larguèche, Dalenda 26
laundry 8, 9–10, 12
al-Lawāṭī, Ibrīk 58
Lettuce and Flowers (*khass wa-nuwwar*) 17–18
Libyan Studies Center (Tripoli) 49–50
literacy amongst Jews in late Ottoman Libya 19, 20, 21–2

al-Mabrūk, Ruqiyya 60
Maddy-Weitzman, Bruce 95, 96, 104n2
Mahsan, Ahmad 34
marriage 27, 33–4, 37, 51; among Jews in late Ottoman period 13, 15–19, 22, 30; pastoral societies in Cyrenaica 51–2; *see also* dowries; weddings; wives
al-Masārī, Fāṭima Muḥammad Būnajī 58
al-Masārī, Muḥammad Būnajī 59
Massey, Doreen 101
McDougall, James 92–3
memory 2, 50, 69, 70, 79, 83, 95; transcultural 1, 3, 67–89; *see also* remembering
Memory Studies 3, 69
menstruation 7, 8, 50
midwifery 12, 83
Miller, Susan 97
Mislata 8, 9, 10, 11
mnemonic processes 67, 69, 70, 71, 74–84
modesty 7–8, 50, 58, 62
Montana, Ismael 36
morality 28, 29, 30–1, 34
Morocco/Moroccans 78, 90, 92–3, 95, 96, 103, 104n1
Morzuk 31
Mubarak, Hosni 93
mujāhidīn 2, 47, 49, 52–5, 57, 58, 59, 60, 64
al-Mukhtār, Fāṭima ʿUmar 58
al-Mukhtār, ʿUmar 49, 58–9, 61
municipal councils 28, 31, 32, 34
Muñoz, José Esteban 99
music, Amazigh 90–106
Muslims 51, 52, 70, 72, 74, 77, 78; in late Ottoman period Libya 6, 9, 10, 11, 13, 15, 18, 21, 22
Mussolini, Benito 55

Nashat, Guity 25–6
nationalism 49, 55, 74, 76, 84, 94, 101–2, *102*
natron 8, 10, 12
nomads 49, 51–2; *see also* Bedouin
Noon Arts Project 3
notables 25, 27, 28, 30, 31, 32, 33–4, 36–7, 38, 55
Nünning, Ansgar 70

Obeidi, Amal 26
oral history 2, 47, 48, 49–50, 67–84
oral poetry 21–2
orientalist clichés 25, 34, 35
Othmana, Aziza 33
Ottoman period: late, Jews in 5–23; Tripoli in 24–46

Paggi, Giannetto 72
Palestine 25, 34, 73
pan-Arabism 94, 105n8
Passover 8, 9, 10, 11, 17
patriarchy 25, 26, 40, 48, 64
Peirce, Leslie 29
Peters, Emrys L. 50, 51
petitions 15, 24–40
poetry 21–2, 95, 98
policing 39, 100
Portelli, Alessandro 50
postcolonial period 1–2, 68, 72, 74, 94, 95
property ownership 20, 28, 51–2
prostitution 18, 23n3, 24–5, 27, 28–9, 30, 38–40; *see also* concubines
purification 7–8
Purim festival 14–15, 20

al-Qabṭān, Mubrūka 52, 54
Qaddafi *see* Gaddafi (Qaddafi), Muammar
Qaramanli dynasty 15, 25, 35, 37
al-Qarqani (*sheikh al-bilâd*) 36, 37–8, 39–40
al-Qatalā, Adm al-Hāyin Sulayman 62

racism 103–4
Rafeq, Abdul-Karim 28
rape 18, 38, 58, 64
reconquista 55–6
remembering 67–84; *see also* memory
repudiation 34, 38
reputation 29, 33, 36, 38
resistance to Italian colonial rule 47–66
Rome 68, 71, 72, 74, 79, 82
Rossetto, Piera 70

rural women: colonial period 52; late Ottoman period 5, 6–7, 8, 9–11, 12, 13, 15–16, 22; Ottoman Tripoli 35, 38

Sabbath 8, 9, 13, 14, 15, 20, 21
Salim, Asma 103
al-Sanūsī, Idrīs al-Mahdī 55
Sanusi movement (*Sanūsiyya*) 55
Second World War 73, 74–5
Sephardi Jews 69–70, 77, 79
Serbia 90, 92, 96, 97, 101
sexual abuse 37, 38, 39, 55, 58, 64; *see also* rape
sexuality 29, 50
Shahhat 52, 55
Simon, Rachel 2, 5–23, 30
Siwa (Egypt) 58
slavery 24–5, 28–9, 30, 36–8, 39, 58
Sonbol, Amira 26
Spadaro, Barbara 1–4, 29, 67–89
Spain 25, 82
Sterne, Jonathan 101
Strangelove, Michael 101
Strobel, Margaret 25
Sufism 55
Sulaymān, Jamīla Saʿīd 52, 53, 54, 56, 57, 61–2, 63
Sunni Islam 51
synagogues 15, 19–21

al-Tabalqī, al-Sabir Muḥammad Yūsif 53
Takfarinas, Amazighi 103
Tamazight language 90, 91, 92, 94, 95–7, 98–9, 100, 101, 104
tanzimat era 25, 31, 33, 40
Tayeb, Leila 90–106
Taysir, Ben Musa 33, 35
Thompson, Elisabeth 29
tifinagh writing system 96, 97, 100
Tobruk 55, 93
torture 57, 63
trade, women in 10, 35–6
transcultural memory 1, 3, 67–89
Tripoli 55, 72, 90–1, 100, 103; Jewish families in colonial era 67–8, 71, 72, 73–5, 76, 77, 78, 80–1, 82, 83, 84; in late Ottoman period 8, 10, 11–12, 13, 14, 15, 16–17, 18, 19, 20, 21, 22; Libyan Studies Center 49–50; in Ottoman period 24–46
Tripolitania 7, 15, 25, 47, 50, 55–6, 60
Tuareg 96, 103
Tucker, Judith 25–6, 34
Tunisia/Tunisians 25, 26, 33, 35, 36, 63, 72, 90, 91, 92, 93, 98, 100, 103, 104n1

al-ʿUbaydī, Massʿūd 57
UK (United Kingdom) 67, 68, 71
USSME (Ufficio Storico dello Stato Maggiore dell'Esercito) 50
al-Ustā,' Mohammad 27

Vansina, Jan 49–50
'Veil of shame' 16–17
Vidal-Naquet, Pierre 57
violence 29–30, 37, 40; and gender in the Italian period 47–66

Wādī al-Shabriq wa al-Muḥaja, battle of 54, 61
waqf system 32, 33, 37
water drawing 10–11, 13, 15–16, 51, 53
weddings 8, 16–17, 18, 27, 34; *see also* marriage
wells 10–11, 56, 60; *see also* water drawing
widows 20, 24–5, 28–9, 33, 35, 36, 38, 40, 59
wives 18, 24–5, 28, 33–4, 35, 37
wood chopping 10, 11–12, 51, 53
work, women's: Jews in late Ottoman period 7, 8–13, 22–3, 30; in Ottoman Tripoli 30, 34–6; during the resistance 51, 53
Wright, John 36

Yeaw, Katrina 1–4, 47–66
Yefreb 8
Yom Kippur 6, 15, 20
Young, Sara B. 70
YouTube 98–9, 101

Zanzur 7
Zliten 20
Zohra, Lila 35–6
Zuwara 94, 96, 97–8, 101

Milton Keynes UK
Ingram Content Group UK Ltd.
UKHW020255190324
439716UK00003B/23